THE ESSENTIAL TOWER AIR FRYER COOKBOOK UK 2024

1800 Days of Quick, Delicious Recipes for Beginners

Nicole Williams

CONTENTS

INTRODUCTION

The Essential Tower Air Fryer Cookbook UK 2024: 1800 Days of Quick, Delicious Recipes for Beginners

Unlock the full potential of your Tower Air Fryer with this comprehensive cookbook tailored for UK home cooks! Whether you're new to air frying or looking to expand your recipe repertoire, this guide is packed with 1800 days worth of mouthwatering meals that are both quick to prepare and bursting with flavour.

Inside, you'll discover:

- Easy-to-follow recipes using ingredients readily available in UK supermarkets
- A wide variety of dishes for every meal and occasion
- Tips and tricks to master your Tower Air Fryer
- Nutritional information to help you make informed choices

Explore delicious recipes including:

- Hearty British breakfasts
- Succulent poultry dishes
- Tender meat creations
- Flavourful fish and seafood
- Crispy vegetable sides
- Quick snacks and appetisers
- Indulgent desserts

From classic favourites to innovative new ideas, this cookbook will help you create healthier versions of your favourite fried foods without sacrificing taste. Say goodbye to excess oil and hello to crispy, golden perfection!

Perfect for busy families, health-conscious cooks, and anyone looking to simplify their meal prep. With 1800 days of recipes, you'll never run out of inspiration!

Ready to revolutionise your cooking? Click "Buy Now" to start your air frying journey today!

Bread And Breakfast

Sweet Potato & Mushroom Hash

Servings: 6 | Prep Time: 10 Minutes | Cooking Time: 35 Minutes

Ingredients:

- 2 peeled sweet potatoes, cubed
- 115-g baby Bella mushrooms, diced
- 1/2 red bell pepper, diced
- 1/2 red onion, diced
- 2 tbsp olive oil
- 1 garlic clove, minced
- Salt and pepper to taste
- 1/2 tbsp chopped marjoram

Directions:

1. Preheat air fryer to 190°C/380°F.
2. Place all ingredients in a bowl and toss to coat veggies.
3. Pour into air fryer basket.
4. Bake for 8-10 mins, shake, then cook 8-10 more mins until tender.
5. Serve and enjoy!

Variations & Ingredients Tips:

- Add diced ham, bacon or chorizo.
- Use sweet or hot paprika, or smoked paprika for extra flavor.
- Top with a fried egg or avocado slices.

Per Serving: Calories: 98; Total Fat: 5g; Saturated Fat: 1g; Cholesterol: 0mg; Sodium: 33mg; Total Carbs: 13g; Dietary Fiber: 2g; Total Sugars: 3g; Protein: 2g

Morning Apple Biscuits

Servings: 6 | Prep Time: 5 Minutes | Cooking Time: 15 Minutes

Ingredients:

- 1 apple, grated
- 1 cup oat flour
- 2 tbsp honey
- 1/4 cup peanut butter
- 1/3 cup raisins
- 1/2 tsp ground cinnamon

Directions:

1. Preheat air fryer to 175°C/350°F.
2. Combine apple, flour, honey, peanut butter, raisins and cinnamon in a bowl.
3. Form into balls and flatten slightly.
4. Place on parchment paper in air fryer basket.
5. Bake for 9 minutes until lightly browned.
6. Serve warm.

Variations & Ingredients Tips:

- Use almond or cashew butter instead of peanut.
- Add chopped nuts or chocolate chips.
- Drizzle with maple syrup or dust with powdered sugar.

Per Serving: Calories: 140; Total Fat: 6g; Saturated Fat: 1g; Cholesterol: 0mg; Sodium: 45mg; 19g; Dietary Fiber: 3g; Sugars: 9g; Protein: 4g

Mushroom & Cavolo Nero Egg Muffins

Servings: 6 | Prep Time: 10 Minutes | Cooking Time: 20 Minutes

Ingredients:

- 225g baby Bella mushrooms, sliced
- 6 eggs, beaten
- 1 garlic clove, minced
- Salt and pepper to taste
- 1/2 tsp chili powder
- 1 cup cavolo nero (Tuscan kale), shredded
- 2 scallions, diced

Directions:

1. Preheat air fryer to 160°C/320°F.
2. Place eggs, garlic, salt, pepper and chili powder in a bowl and beat well combined.
3. Fold in mushrooms, cavolo nero and scallions.
4. Divide mixture between greased muffin cups and place in air fryer basket.
5. Bake for 12-15 minutes until eggs are set.
6. Cool 5 minutes before serving.

Variations & Ingredients Tips:

- Use different greens like spinach or chard.
- Add diced ham, bacon or cheese.
- Cook in oven-safe ramekins if air fryer cups are too small.

Per Serving: Calories: 75; Total Fat: 4g; Saturated Fat: 1g; Cholesterol: 155mg; Sodium: 90mg; Total Carbs: 4g; Dietary Fiber: 1g; Sugars: 2g; Protein: 6g

Sweet And Spicy Pumpkin Scones

Servings: 8 | Prep Time: 20 Minutes Cooking Time: 8 Minutes

Ingredients:

- 2 cups all-purpose flour
- 3 tablespoons packed brown sugar
- 1/2 teaspoon baking powder
- 1/4 teaspoon baking soda
- 1/2 teaspoon kosher salt
- 1/2 teaspoon ground cinnamon
- 1/4 teaspoon ground ginger
- 1/4 teaspoon ground cardamom
- 4 tablespoons cold unsalted butter
- 1/2 cup plus 2 tablespoons pumpkin puree, divided
- 4 tablespoons milk, divided
- 1 large egg
- 1 cup powdered sugar

Directions:

1. In a large bowl, mix flour, brown sugar, baking powder, baking soda, salt, cinnamon, ginger, and cardamom. Cut in the butter until crumbly.
2. In a small bowl, whisk 1/2 cup pumpkin puree, 2 tablespoons milk, and the egg. Pour into dry ingredients and stir to combine.
3. Form dough into a ball, roll out 1.3-cm thick and cut into 8 wedges.
4. Bake at 180°C/360°F for 8-10 minutes until cooked through.
5. Make glaze by whisking 1 cup powdered sugar, 2 tablespoons pumpkin puree, 2 tablespoons milk. Drizzle over cooled scones.

Variations & Ingredients Tips:

- Add chopped pecans or raisins to the dough.
- Use buttermilk instead of regular milk for extra tang.
- Brush with melted butter instead of the glaze.

Per Serving: Calories: 275; Total Fat: 8g; Saturated Fat: 5g; Cholesterol: 41mg; Sodium: 180mg; Total Carbs: 47g; Dietary Fiber: 1g; Total Sugars: 25g; Protein: 4g

Crispy Samosa Rolls

Servings: 4 | Prep Time: 20 Minutes | Cooking Time: 30 Minutes

Ingredients:

- ⅔ cup canned peas
- 4 scallions, finely sliced
- 2 cups grated potatoes
- 2 tablespoons lemon juice
- 1 teaspoon ground ginger
- 1 teaspoon curry powder
- 1 teaspoon Garam masala
- ¼ cup chickpea flour
- 1 tablespoon tahini
- 8 rice paper wrappers

Directions:

1. Preheat air fryer to 180°C/350°F.
2. Mix the peas, scallions, potatoes, lemon juice, ginger, curry powder, Garam masala, and chickpea flour in a bowl.
3. In another bowl, whisk tahini and 80 ml of water until combined. Set aside on a plate.
4. Submerge the rice wrappers, one by one, into the tahini mixture until they begin to soften and set aside on a plate.
5. Fill each wrap with ⅓ cup of the veggie mixture and wrap them into a roll.
6. Bake for 15 minutes until golden brown and crispy, turning once.
7. Serve right away.

Variations & Ingredients Tips:

- Use different types of vegetables, such as carrots or sweet potatoes, for a variety of flavors and textures.
- Add some chopped nuts or raisins to the filling for extra flavor and crunch.
- Serve the samosa rolls with a side of chutney or yogurt sauce for dipping.

Per Serving: Calories: 230; Total Fat: 5g; Saturated Fat: 1g; Cholesterol: 0mg; Sodium: 160mg; Total Carbs: 41g; Fiber: 6g; Sugars: 5g; Protein: 7g

Canadian Bacon & Cheese Sandwich

Servings: 1 | Prep Time: 5 Minutes | Cooking Time: 30 Minutes

Ingredients:

- 1 English muffin, halved
- 1 egg
- 1 Canadian bacon slice
- 1 slice provolone cheese

Directions:

1. Preheat air fryer to 177°C/350°F. Put muffin halves, cut-side up, and bacon slice in air fryer basket. Bake 5 minutes.
2. Flip muffins and bacon. Place cheese slice on muffins.
3. Beat egg in a heatproof bowl. Add bowl to basket next to sandwich.
4. Bake 15 more minutes until cheese melts, bacon crisps and egg sets.
5. Assemble sandwich with bacon, egg and cheese between muffin halves.

Variations & Ingredients Tips:

- Use different cheese like cheddar or swiss.
- Add sliced tomato or avocado to the sandwich.
- Cook extra eggs to make it a double decker.

Per Serving: Calories: 385; Total Fat: 20g; Saturated Fat: 10g; Cholesterol: 265mg; Sodium: 910mg; Total Carbs: 29g; Dietary Fiber: 1g; Total Sugars: 3g; Protein: 24g

Cherry-apple Oatmeal Cups

Servings: 2 | Prep Time: 5 Minutes | Cooking Time: 20 Minutes

Ingredients:

- 2/3 cup rolled oats
- 1 cored apple, diced
- 4 pitted cherries, diced
- ½ tsp ground cinnamon
- ¾ cup milk

Directions:

1. Preheat air fryer to 177°C/350°F.
2. In a heatproof bowl, mix oats, apple, cherries and cinnamon.
3. Stir in milk.
4. Place bowl in air fryer basket and bake 6 minutes.
5. Stir well and bake 6 more minutes until fruit is soft.
6. Serve cooled.

Variations & Ingredients Tips:

- Use any variety of fresh or frozen berries.
- Substitute almond or oat milk for dairy milk.
- Top with nuts, seeds, honey or nut butter before serving.

Per Serving: Calories: 210; Total Fat: 3g; Saturated Fat: 1g; Cholesterol: 5mg; Sodium: 35mg; Total Carbs: 39g; Dietary Fiber: 5g; Total Sugars: 15g; Protein: 6g

French Toast Sticks

Servings: 4 | Prep Time: 10 Minutes | Cooking Time: 8 Minutes

Ingredients:

- 2 eggs
- ¼ cup half-and-half
- ½ teaspoon vanilla extract
- 6 slices wheat bread, cut into 2.5 cm strips
- 1 teaspoon ground cinnamon
- 2 tablespoons granulated sugar
- Maple syrup or pureed strawberries for serving

Directions:

1. In a 20 x 30 cm casserole dish, whisk together the eggs, half-and-half, and vanilla. Lay the strips of bread into the baking dish and flip around. Allow the bread to soak up the egg mixture for 10 minutes.
2. Meanwhile, in a small bowl, stir together the cinnamon and sugar.
3. Place the soaked bread strips into the air fryer basket, not touching one another. Spray with cooking spray and sprinkle the cinnamon and sugar mixture onto the bread sticks.
4. Air fry the French toast sticks at 190°C/370°F for 8 minutes. Cook in batches, as needed.
5. Serve with maple syrup or pureed strawberries.

Variations & Ingredients Tips:

- Use brioche, challah or French bread instead of wheat bread for a richer flavor.
- Add a pinch of nutmeg or cardamom to the cinnamon sugar mixture.
- Dip the sticks in a fruit compote, chocolate sauce or caramel for a decadent twist.

Per Serving: Calories: 176; Total Fat: 5g; Saturated Fat: 2g; Cholesterol: 98mg; Sodium: 250mg; Total Carbs: 27g; Dietary Fiber: 2g; Total Sugars: 10g; Protein: 7g

Goat Cheese, Beet, And Kale Frittata

Servings: 6 | Prep Time: 10 Minutes | Cooking Time: 20 Minutes

Ingredients:

- 6 large eggs
- ½ teaspoon garlic powder
- ¼ teaspoon black pepper
- ¼ teaspoon salt
- 1 cup chopped kale
- 1 cup cooked and chopped red beets
- 85 g crumbled goat cheese

Directions:

1. Preheat the air fryer to 160°C/320°F.
2. In a medium bowl, whisk the eggs with the garlic powder, pepper, and salt. Mix in the kale, beets, and goat cheese.
3. Spray an oven-safe 18 cm springform pan with cooking spray. Pour the egg mixture into the pan and place it in the air fryer basket.
4. Cook for 20 minutes, or until the internal temperature reaches 63°C/145°F.
5. When the frittata is cooked, let it set for 5 minutes before removing from the pan.
6. Slice and serve immediately.

Variations & Ingredients Tips:

- Use Swiss chard, spinach or arugula instead of kale.
- Swap goat cheese for feta, ricotta or cream cheese.
- Add some sun-dried tomatoes, olives or roasted red peppers for Mediterranean flair.

Per Serving: Calories: 135; Total Fat: 9g; Saturated Fat: 4g; Cholesterol: 196mg; Sodium: 265mg; Total Carbs: 4g; Dietary Fiber: 1g; Total Sugars: 2g; Protein: 10g

Aromatic Mushroom Omelet

Servings: 4 | Prep Time: 10 Minutes | Cooking Time: 30 Minutes

Ingredients:

- 6 eggs
- 2 tbsp milk
- ½ yellow onion, diced
- ½ cup diced mushrooms
- 2 tbsp chopped parsley
- 1 tsp dried oregano
- 1 tbsp chopped chives
- ½ tbsp chopped dill
- ½ cup grated Gruyère cheese

Directions:

1. Preheat air fryer to 177°C/350°F.
2. Beat eggs in a medium bowl, then add milk, onion, mushrooms, oregano, chives, dill and cheese. Stir until combined.
3. Pour mixture into a greased baking pan and place in air fryer basket.
4. Bake for 18-20 minutes until eggs are set.
5. Top with parsley and serve.

Variations & Ingredients Tips:

- Use different cheese like cheddar or feta
- Add cooked bacon, ham or sausage
- Cook in individual ramekins for single-serve portions

Per Serving: Calories: 170; Total Fat: 11g; Saturated Fat: 5g; Cholesterol: 280mg; Sodium: 225mg; Total Carbs: 4g; Dietary Fiber: 1g; Total Sugars: 2g; Protein: 13g

Lemon-blueberry Morning Bread

Servings: 2 | Prep Time: 5 Minutes | Cooking Time: 15 Minutes

Ingredients:

- 60 g flour
- 30 g powdered sugar
- ½ teaspoon baking powder
- ⅛ teaspoon salt
- 2 tablespoons butter, melted
- 1 egg
- ½ teaspoon gelatin
- ½ teaspoon vanilla extract
- 1 teaspoon lemon zest
- ½ cup blueberries

Directions:

1. Preheat air fryer to 150°C/300°F. Mix the flour, sugar, baking powder, and salt in a bowl. In another bowl, whisk the butter, egg, gelatin, lemon zest, vanilla extract, and blueberries. Add egg mixture to flour mixture and stir until smooth. Spoon mixture into a pizza pan. Place pan in the frying basket and Bake for 10 minutes. Let sit for 5 minutes before slicing. Serve immediately.

Variations & Ingredients Tips:

- Use raspberries, blackberries or chopped strawberries instead of blueberries.
- Add some poppy seeds or chopped nuts to the batter for texture.
- Top with a dollop of lemon curd or cream cheese frosting.

Per Serving: Calories: 320; Total Fat: 14g; Saturated Fat: 8g; Cholesterol: 123mg; Sodium: 298mg; Total Carbs: 44g; Dietary Fiber: 2g; Total Sugars: 23g; Protein: 6g

English Scones

Servings: 8 | Prep Time: 15 Minutes | Cooking Time: 8 Minutes

Ingredients:

- 2 cups all-purpose flour
- 1 tablespoon baking powder
- ½ teaspoon salt
- 2 tablespoons sugar
- ¼ cup unsalted butter
- 158 ml plus 15 ml whole milk, divided

Directions:

1. Preheat the air fryer to 190°C/380°F.
2. In a large bowl, whisk together the flour, baking powder, salt, and sugar. Using a pastry blender or your fingers, cut in the butter until pea-size crumbles appear. Make a well in the center and pour in 158 ml of the milk. Quickly mix the batter until a ball forms. Knead the dough 3 times.
3. Place the dough onto a floured surface and, using your hands or a rolling pin, flatten the dough until it's 2 cm thick. Using a biscuit cutter or drinking glass, cut out 10 circles, reforming the dough and flattening as needed to use up the batter.
4. Brush the tops lightly with the remaining 15 ml of milk.
5. Place the scones into the air fryer basket. Cook for 8 minutes or until golden brown and cooked in the center.

Variations & Ingredients Tips:

- Add some dried currants, chocolate chips or chopped candied ginger to the dough.
- Sprinkle the tops with coarse sugar or brush with cream before baking.
- Serve with clotted cream, lemon curd or your favorite jam.

Per Serving: Calories: 218; Total Fat: 8g; Saturated Fat: 5g; Cholesterol: 21mg; Sodium: 292mg; Total Carbs: 32g; Dietary Fiber: 1g; Total Sugars: 4g; Protein: 5g

Thai Turkey Sausage Patties

Servings: 4 | Prep Time: 10 Minutes | Cooking Time: 30 Minutes

Ingredients:

- 340g turkey sausage
- 1 tsp onion powder
- 1 tsp dried coriander
- ¼ tsp Thai curry paste
- ¼ tsp red pepper flakes
- Salt and pepper to taste

Directions:

1. Preheat air fryer to 175°C/350°F.
2. Place the sausage, onion powder, coriander, curry paste, red pepper flakes, salt, and black pepper in a large bowl and mix well.
3. Form into eight patties.

4. Arrange the patties on the greased air fryer basket and air fry for 10 minutes, flipping once halfway through.
5. Once cooked, transfer patties to a plate and serve hot.

Variations & Ingredients Tips:

- Use ground turkey or chicken instead of sausage.
- Add grated ginger or lemongrass for more Thai flavor.
- Serve with a sweet chili sauce for dipping.

Per Serving: Calories: 195; Total Fat: 12g; Saturated Fat: 3g; Cholesterol: 70mg; Sodium: 540mg; Total Carbs: 2g; Dietary Fiber: 1g; Total Sugars: 0g; Protein: 20g

Apple & Turkey Breakfast Sausages

Servings: 4 | Prep Time: 10 Minutes | Cooking Time: 15 Minutes

Ingredients:

- ½ tsp coriander seeds, crushed
- 1 tbsp chopped rosemary
- 1 tbsp chopped thyme
- Salt and pepper to taste
- 1 tsp fennel seeds, crushed
- ¾ tsp smoked paprika
- ½ tsp garlic powder
- ½ tsp shallot powder
- ⅛ tsp red pepper flakes
- 454g ground turkey
- ½ cup minced apples

Directions:

1. Combine all of the seasonings in a bowl. Add turkey and apple and blend seasonings in well with your hands. Form patties about 7.5cm in diameter and 0.6cm thick.
2. Preheat air fryer to 205°C/400°F. Arrange patties in a single layer on the greased frying basket. Air Fry for 10 minutes, flipping once until brown and cooked through. Serve.

Variations & Ingredients Tips:

- Use ground chicken or pork instead of turkey
- Add dried fruits like cranberries or apricots
- Mix in breadcrumbs or oats for a binder

Per Serving: Calories: 190; Total Fat: 8g; Saturated Fat: 2g; Cholesterol: 65mg; Sodium: 210mg; Total Carbs: 7g; Dietary Fiber: 1g; Total Sugars: 3g; Protein: 23g

Lemon Monkey Bread

Servings: 4 | Prep Time: 10 Minutes | Cooking Time: 15 Minutes

Ingredients:

- 1 can refrigerated biscuits
- ¼ cup white sugar
- 3 tablespoons brown sugar
- ½ teaspoon ground cinnamon
- 1 lemon, zested
- ¼ teaspoon ground nutmeg
- 3 tablespoons melted butter

Directions:

1. Preheat air fryer to 175°C/350°F. Take the biscuits out of the can and separate them. Cut each biscuit into 4 equal pieces. In a bowl, mix white sugar, brown sugar, lemon zest, cinnamon, and nutmeg. Have the melted butter nearby. Dip each biscuit piece into the butter, then roll into the cinnamon sugar until coated. Place in a baking pan. Bake in the air fryer until golden brown, 6-9 minutes. Let cool for 5 minutes before serving as the sugar will be hot.

Variations & Ingredients Tips:

- Add some chopped pecans or walnuts to the sugar mixture for crunch.
- Drizzle with a lemon glaze made of powdered sugar and lemon juice.
- Serve with fresh berries and whipped cream for a decadent treat.

Per Serving: Calories: 397; Total Fat: 18g; Saturated Fat: 6g; Cholesterol: 16mg; Sodium: 781mg; Total Carbs: 56g; Dietary Fiber: 1g; Total Sugars: 27g; Protein: 5g

Blueberry French Toast Sticks

Servings: 4 | Prep Time: 10 Minutes | Cooking Time: 20 Minutes

Ingredients:

- 3 bread slices, cut into strips
- 1 tbsp butter, melted
- 2 eggs
- 1 tbsp milk
- 1 tbsp sugar
- ½ tsp vanilla extract
- 1 cup fresh blueberries
- 1 tbsp lemon juice

Directions:

1. Preheat air fryer to 193°C/380°F.
2. Brush bread strips with melted butter.
3. Whisk eggs, milk, sugar and vanilla. Dip bread in egg mixture and place on a rack to drip off excess.
4. Air fry bread 5-7 minutes, flipping once, until golden brown.
5. In a bowl, mash blueberries with lemon juice to make a sauce.
6. Drizzle blueberry sauce over the warm French toast sticks and serve immediately.

Variations & Ingredients Tips:

- Use challah or brioche bread for extra richness.
- Add a pinch of cinnamon to the egg mixture.
- Top with powdered sugar or maple syrup.

Per Serving: Calories: 145; Total Fat: 5g; Saturated Fat: 2g; Cholesterol: 110mg; Sodium: 160mg; Total Carbs: 21g; Dietary Fiber: 2g; Total Sugars: 10g; Protein: 5g

Morning Burrito

Servings: 4 | Prep Time: 10 Minutes | Cooking Time: 15 Minutes

Ingredients:

- 56-g cheddar cheese, torn into pieces
- 2 hard-boiled eggs, chopped
- 1 avocado, chopped
- 1 red bell pepper, chopped
- 3 tbsp salsa
- 4 flour tortillas

Directions:

1. Whisk the eggs, avocado, red bell pepper, salsa, and cheese.
2. Pour the tortillas on a clean surface and divide the egg mix between them.
3. Fold the edges and roll up; poke a toothpick through so they hold.
4. Preheat air fryer to 200°C/390°F.
5. Place the burritos in the frying basket and Air Fry for 3-5 minutes until crispy and golden.
6. Serve hot.

Variations & Ingredients Tips:

- Add cooked potatoes, bacon or chorizo to the filling.
- Use whole wheat or spinach tortillas for extra nutrition.
- Serve with sour cream, guacamole or extra salsa on the side.

Per Serving: Calories: 320; Total Fat: 18g; Saturated Fat: 6g; Cholesterol: 155mg; Sodium: 480mg; Total Carbs: 28g; Dietary Fiber: 5g; Sugars: 3g; Protein: 12g

Bagels With Avocado & Tomatoes

Servings: 2 | Prep Time: 20 Minutes | Cooking Time: 35 Minutes

Ingredients:

- 2/3 cup all-purpose flour
- ½ tsp active dry yeast
- 1/3 cup Greek yogurt
- 8 cherry tomatoes
- 1 ripe avocado
- 1 tbsp lemon juice
- 2 tbsp chopped red onions
- Black pepper to taste

Directions:

1. Preheat air fryer to 205°C/400°F. Beat flour, yeast, and yogurt into a dough, adding more flour if needed. Make 2 balls.
2. Roll each into a 23cm strip and form rings, pressing ends together to make 2 bagels. Soak in hot water 1 min.
3. Drain and let bagels rise 15 mins in fryer. Bake 5 mins, flip, top with tomatoes and bake 5 more mins.
4. Make guacamole: Mash avocado flesh with lemon juice and onions.
5. Cut bagels in half and spread with guacamole. Top with baked tomatoes and black pepper.

Variations & Ingredients Tips:

- Use whole wheat or alternative flour for the bagels.
- Mix chopped jalapeño or cilantro into the guacamole.
- Top with sliced hard boiled eggs for extra protein.

Per Serving: Calories: 410; Total Fat: 12g; Saturated Fat: 2g; Cholesterol: 0mg; Sodium: 135mg; Total Carbs: 65g; Dietary Fiber: 9g; Total Sugars: 5g; Protein: 13g

Chicken Scotch Eggs

Servings: 4 | Prep Time: 15 Minutes | Cooking Time: 25 Minutes

Ingredients:

- 450 g ground chicken
- 2 teaspoons Dijon mustard
- 2 teaspoons grated yellow onion
- 1 tablespoon chopped chives
- 1 tablespoon chopped parsley
- ⅛ teaspoon ground nutmeg
- 1 lemon, zested
- Salt and pepper to taste
- 4 hard-boiled eggs, peeled
- 1 egg, beaten
- 1 cup bread crumbs
- 2 teaspoons olive oil

Directions:

1. Preheat air fryer to 180°C/350°F.
2. In a bowl, mix the ground chicken, mustard, onion, chives, parsley, nutmeg, salt, lemon zest and pepper. Shape into 4 oval balls and form the balls evenly around the boiled eggs.
3. Submerge them in the beaten egg and dip in the crumbs. Brush with olive oil.
4. Place the scotch eggs in the frying basket and Air Fry for 14 minutes, flipping once.
5. Serve hot.

Variations & Ingredients Tips:

- Use different types of ground meat, such as turkey or pork, for a variety of flavors.
- Add some chopped bacon or sun-dried tomatoes to the meat mixture for extra flavor.
- Serve the scotch eggs with a side of mustard or hot sauce for dipping.

Per Serving: Calories: 360; Total Fat: 20g; Saturated Fat: 5g; Cholesterol: 305mg; Sodium: 420mg; Total Carbs: 16g; Fiber: 1g; Sugars: 1g; Protein: 30g

Chili Hash Browns

Servings: 4 | Prep Time: 10 Minutes | Cooking Time: 45 Minutes

Ingredients:

- 1 tablespoon ancho chili powder
- 1 tablespoon chipotle powder
- 2 teaspoons ground cumin
- 2 teaspoons smoked paprika
- 1 teaspoon garlic powder
- 1 teaspoon cayenne pepper
- Salt and pepper to taste
- 2 peeled russet potatoes, grated
- 2 tablespoons olive oil
- ⅓ cup chopped onion
- 3 garlic cloves, minced

Directions:

1. Preheat the air fryer to 200°C/400°F.
2. Combine chili powder, cumin, paprika, garlic powder, chipotle, cayenne, and black pepper in a small bowl, then pour into a glass jar with a lid and store in a cool, dry place.
3. Add the olive oil, onion, and garlic to a cake pan, put it in the air fryer, and Bake for 3 minutes.
4. Put the grated potatoes in a bowl and sprinkle with 2 teaspoons of the spice mixture, toss and add them to the cake pan along with the onion mix.
5. Bake for 20-23 minutes, stirring once or until the potatoes are crispy and golden. Season with salt and serve.

Variations & Ingredients Tips:

- Use different types of potatoes, such as sweet potatoes or Yukon Gold, for a variety of flavors and textures.
- Add some diced bell peppers or jalapeños to the hash browns for extra vegetables and heat.
- Serve the hash browns with a side of salsa or sour cream for a Mexican-inspired breakfast.

Per Serving: Calories: 220; Total Fat: 7g; Saturated Fat: 1g; Cholesterol: 0mg; Sodium: 50mg; Total Carbs: 36g; Fiber: 4g; Sugars: 2g; Protein: 5g

Appetizers And Snacks

Cauliflower "tater" Tots

Servings: 6 | Prep Time: 20 Minutes | Cooking Time: 10 Minutes

Ingredients:

- 1 head of cauliflower
- 2 eggs
- ¼ cup all-purpose flour*
- ½ cup grated Parmesan cheese
- 1 teaspoon salt
- freshly ground black pepper
- vegetable or olive oil, in a spray bottle

Directions:

1. Grate the head of cauliflower with a box grater or finely chop it in a food processor. You should have about 3½ cups. Place the chopped cauliflower in the center of a clean kitchen towel and twist the towel tightly to squeeze all the water out of the cauliflower. (This can be done in two batches to make it easier to drain all the water from the cauliflower.)
2. Place the squeezed cauliflower in a large bowl. Add the eggs, flour, Parmesan cheese, salt and freshly ground black pepper. Shape the cauliflower into small cylinders or "tater tot" shapes, rolling roughly one tablespoon of the mixture at a time. Place the tots on a cookie sheet lined with paper towel to absorb any residual moisture. Spray the cauliflower tots all over with oil.
3. Preheat the air fryer to 200°C/400°F.
4. Air-fry the tots at 200°C/400°F, one layer at a time for 10 minutes, turning them over for the last few minutes of the cooking process for even browning. Season with salt and black pepper. Serve hot with your favorite dipping sauce.

Variations & Ingredients Tips:

- Add some shredded cheese, bacon bits or chopped herbs to the mixture.
- Make them into larger patties for cauliflower hash browns.
- Serve with ketchup, ranch dressing or sriracha mayo for dipping.

Per Serving: Calories: 113; Total Fat: 6g; Saturated Fat: 3g; Cholesterol: 63mg; Sodium: 548mg; Total Carbs: 8g; Dietary Fiber: 3g; Total Sugars: 3g; Protein: 7g

Poppy Seed Mini Hot Dog Rolls

Servings: 4 | Prep Time: 10 Minutes | Cooking Time: 25 Minutes

Ingredients:

- 8 small mini hot dogs
- 8 pastry dough sheets

- 1 tbsp vegetable oil
- 1 tbsp poppy seeds

Directions:

1. Preheat the air fryer to 175°C/350°F. Roll the mini hot dogs into a pastry dough sheet, wrapping them snugly. Brush the rolls with vegetable oil on all sides. Arrange them on the frying basket and sprinkle poppy seeds on top. Bake for 15 minutes until the pastry crust is golden brown. Serve.

Variations & Ingredients Tips:

- Use different types of sausages like bratwurst, Italian sausage, or chorizo for variety.
- Brush the rolls with beaten egg instead of oil for a shinier, golden finish.
- Serve with mustard, ketchup, or your favorite dipping sauce.

Per Serving: Calories: 298; Total Fat: 23g; Saturated Fat: 5g; Cholesterol: 15mg; Sodium: 417mg; Total Carbs: 17g; Dietary Fiber: 1g; Total Sugars: 1g; Protein: 6g

Asian Five-spice Wings

Servings: 4 | Prep Time: 5 Minutes | Cooking Time: 15 Minutes

Ingredients:

- 900 g chicken wings
- ½ cup Asian-style salad dressing
- 2 tablespoons Chinese five-spice powder

Directions:

1. Cut off wing tips and discard or freeze for stock. Cut remaining wing pieces in two at the joint.
2. Place wing pieces in a large sealable plastic bag. Pour in the Asian dressing, seal bag, and massage the marinade into the wings until well coated. Refrigerate for at least an hour.
3. Remove wings from bag, drain off excess marinade, and place wings in air fryer basket.
4. Cook at 180°C/360°F for 15 minutes or until juices run clear. About halfway through cooking time, shake the basket or stir wings for more even cooking.
5. Transfer cooked wings to plate in a single layer. Sprinkle half of the Chinese five-spice powder on the wings, turn, and sprinkle other side with remaining seasoning.

Variations & Ingredients Tips:

- Use your favorite Asian-inspired salad dressing or marinade.
- Serve with a hoisin or soy-ginger dipping sauce.
- Toss cooked wings in a sticky Asian bbq sauce.

Per Serving: Calories: 511; Total Fat: 32g; Saturated Fat: 8g; Cholesterol: 191mg; Sodium: 787mg; Total Carbs: 10g; Dietary Fiber: 2g; Total Sugars: 5g; Protein: 44g

Maple Loaded Sweet Potatoes

Servings: 4 | Prep Time: 5 Minutes | Cooking Time: 45 Minutes

Ingredients:

- 4 sweet potatoes
- 2 tbsp butter
- 2 tbsp maple syrup
- 1 tsp cinnamon
- 1 tsp lemon zest
- ½ tsp vanilla extract

Directions:

1. Preheat air fryer to 200°C/390°F. Poke three holes on the top of each sweet potato using a fork. Arrange sweet potatoes in the air fryer and bake for 40 minutes. Remove and let cool for 5 minutes. While the sweet potatoes cool, melt butter and maple syrup together in the microwave for 15-20 seconds. Remove from microwave and stir in cinnamon, lemon zest, and vanilla. When the sweet potatoes are cool enough to handle, cut them open and drizzle the cinnamon butter mixture over each. Serve immediately and enjoy your Maple Loaded Sweet Potatoes!

Variations & Ingredients Tips:

- For a nuttier flavor, add a handful of chopped pecans or walnuts to the butter mixture.
- Substitute honey for the maple syrup if desired.
- For a savory twist, add a pinch of cayenne pepper or smoked paprika to the butter.

Per Serving: Calories: 237; Total Fat: 6g; Saturated Fat: 4g; Cholesterol: 15mg; Sodium: 73mg; Total Carbs: 44g; Dietary Fiber: 5g; Total Sugars: 19g; Protein: 3g

Zucchini Boats With Bacon

Servings: 4 | Prep Time: 15 Minutes | Cooking Time: 35 Minutes

Ingredients:

- 300 g shredded Havarti cheese
- 3 bacon slices
- 2 large zucchini
- Salt and pepper to taste
- ¼ tsp garlic powder
- ¼ tsp sweet paprika
- 8 tsp buttermilk
- 2 tbsp chives, chopped

Directions:

1. Preheat air fryer to 175°C/350°F. Place the bacon in the frying basket and air fry it for 10 minutes, flipping once until crisp. Chop the bacon and set aside. Cut zucchini in half lengthwise and then crosswise so that you have 8 pieces. Scoop out the pulp. Sprinkle with salt, garlic, paprika, and black pepper. Place the zucchini skins in the greased frying basket. Air fry until crisp-tender, 8-10 minutes. Remove the basket and add the Havarti inside each boat and top with bacon. Return stuffed boats to the air fryer and fry

for 2 minutes or until the cheese has melted. Top with buttermilk and chives before serving immediately.

Variations & Ingredients Tips:

- Use cheddar, mozzarella, or goat cheese instead of Havarti for different flavors.
- Add cooked, crumbled sausage, ground beef, or diced ham to the filling for a meatier version.
- Serve with marinara sauce, pesto, or hot sauce for dipping or drizzling.

Per Serving: Calories: 280; Total Fat: 22g; Saturated Fat: 12g; Cholesterol: 69mg; Sodium: 520mg; Total Carbohydrates: 5g; Dietary Fiber: 1g; Total Sugars: 3g; Protein: 17g

Beet Chips With Guacamole

Servings: 4 | Prep Time: 20 Minutes | Cooking Time: 40 Minutes

Ingredients:

- 2 avocados, cubed
- 2 tbsp lime juice
- Celery salt to taste
- 2 beets, peeled
- 2 eggs, beaten
- 1 cup panko bread crumbs
- ½ tsp paprika

Directions:

1. Preheat the air fryer to 190°C/375°F. Mash the avocados, lime juice, and celery salt in a bowl, then pour the guacamole into a serving bowl, cover, and refrigerate. Slice the beets into 7.5 cm long sticks that are 13 mm thick. Beat the eggs in a shallow bowl and combine the panko and paprika on a plate. Dip the fries in the egg, then the panko mixture, coating well. Put the beets in the frying basket and spray with cooking oil, then Air Fry for 18-22 minutes or until crispy and golden. Serve with guacamole.

Variations & Ingredients Tips:

- Use sweet potatoes or carrots instead of beets.
- Season the panko with chili powder or cumin for extra flavor.
- Serve with salsa, queso or ranch dressing for dipping.

Per Serving: Calories: 331; Total Fat: 20g; Saturated Fat: 4g; Cholesterol: 93mg; Sodium: 431mg; Total Carbs: 32g; Dietary Fiber: 8g; Total Sugars: 7g; Protein: 9g

Fried Pickles

Servings: 2 | Prep Time: 10 Minutes | Cooking Time: 15 Minutes

Ingredients:

- 1 egg
- 1 tablespoon milk
- ¼ teaspoon hot sauce
- 2 cups sliced dill pickles, well drained
- ¾ cup breadcrumbs
- oil for misting or cooking spray

Directions:

1. Preheat air fryer to 200°C/390°F.
2. Beat together egg, milk, and hot sauce in a bowl large enough to hold all the pickles.
3. Add pickles to the egg wash and stir well to coat.
4. Place breadcrumbs in a large plastic bag or container with lid.
5. Drain egg wash from pickles and place them in bag with breadcrumbs. Shake to coat.
6. Pile pickles into air fryer basket and spray with oil.
7. Cook for 5 minutes. Shake basket and spray with oil.
8. Cook 5 more minutes. Shake and spray again. Separate any pickles that have stuck together and mist any spots you've missed.
9. Cook for 5 minutes longer or until dark golden brown and crispy.

Variations & Ingredients Tips:

- Use panko breadcrumbs for a crunchier texture.
- Add some garlic powder, onion powder or cayenne pepper to the breading.
- Serve with ranch dressing, blue cheese dip or chipotle mayo for dipping.

Per Serving: Calories: 265; Total Fat: 12g; Saturated Fat: 3g; Cholesterol: 93mg; Sodium: 1769mg; Total Carbs: 29g; Dietary Fiber: 2g; Total Sugars: 5g; Protein: 9g

Cheddar-pimiento Strips

Servings: 4 | Prep Time: 15 Minutes | Cooking Time: 35 Minutes

Ingredients:

- 225 g shredded sharp cheddar cheese
- 1 jar chopped pimientos, including juice
- ¼ cup mayonnaise
- ¼ cup cream cheese
- Salt and pepper to taste
- 1 tsp chopped parsley
- 8 slices sandwich bread
- 4 tbsp butter, melted

Directions:

1. In a bowl, mix the cheddar cheese, cream cheese, pimientos, mayonnaise, salt, parsley and pepper. Let chill covered in the fridge for 30 minutes.
2. Preheat air fryer at 175°C/350°F. Spread pimiento mixture over 4 bread slices, then top with the remaining slices and press down just enough to not smoosh cheese out of sandwiches edges. Brush the top and bottom of each sandwich lightly with melted butter. Place sandwiches in the frying basket and Grill for 6 minutes, flipping once. Slice each sandwich into 16 sections and serve warm.

Variations & Ingredients Tips:

- Use sourdough or rye bread for a tangy flavor.
- Add some chopped green onions or diced jalapenos to the cheese mixture.
- Serve with tomato soup or a green salad on the side.

Per Serving: Calories: 609; Total Fat: 46g; Saturated Fat: 25g; Cholesterol: 97mg; Sodium: 1040mg; Total Carbs: 30g; Dietary Fiber: 2g; Total Sugars: 5g; Protein: 22g

Sweet Apple Fries

Servings: 3 | Prep Time: 15 Minutes | Cooking Time: 8 Minutes

Ingredients:

- 2 medium-size sweet apples, such as Gala or Fuji
- 1 large egg white
- 2 tbsp water
- 1½ cups finely ground gingersnap crumbs (gluten-free, if a concern)
- Vegetable oil spray

Directions:

1. Preheat the air fryer to 190°C/375°F. Peel and core an apple, then cut it into 12 slices (see the headnote for more information). Repeat with more apples as necessary. Whisk the egg white and water in a medium bowl until foamy. Add the apple slices and toss well to coat. Spread the gingersnap crumbs across a dinner plate. Using clean hands, pick up an apple slice, let any excess egg white mixture slip back into the rest, and dredge the slice in the crumbs, coating it lightly but evenly on all sides. Set it aside and continue coating the remaining apple slices. Lightly coat the slices on all sides with vegetable oil spray, then set them curved side down in the basket in one layer. Air-fry undisturbed for 6 minutes, or until browned and crisp. You may need to air-fry the slices for 2 minutes longer if the temperature is at 180°C/360°F. Use kitchen tongs to transfer the slices to a wire rack. Cool for 2 to 3 minutes before serving.

Variations & Ingredients Tips:

- Use different types of apples like Honeycrisp, Granny Smith, or Pink Lady for varied flavors and textures.
- Substitute graham cracker crumbs, crushed vanilla wafers, or cinnamon sugar for the gingersnap crumbs.
- Serve with caramel sauce, whipped cream, or vanilla ice cream for a decadent dessert.

Per Serving: Calories: 223; Total Fat: 2g; Saturated Fat: 0g; Sodium: 201mg; Total Carbohydrates: 49g; Dietary Fiber: 4g; Total Sugars: 29g; Protein: 3g

Hawaiian Ahi Tuna Bowls

Servings: 4 | Prep Time: 15 Minutes | Cooking Time: 20 Minutes

Ingredients:

- 225 g sushi-grade tuna steaks, cubed
- ½ peeled cucumber, diced
- 12 wonton wrappers
- ¾ cup dried beans
- 2 tbsp soy sauce
- 1 tsp toasted sesame oil
- ½ tsp Sriracha sauce
- 1 chili, minced
- 60 g avocado, cubed
- ¼ cup sliced scallions
- 1 tbsp toasted sesame seeds

Directions:

1. Make wonton bowls by placing each wonton wrapper in a foil-lined baking cup. Press gently in the middle and against the sides. Use a light coating of cooking spray. Spoon a heaping tbsp of dried beans into the wonton cup.
2. Preheat air fryer to 140°C/280°F. Place the cups in a single layer on the frying basket. Bake until brown and crispy, 9-11 minutes. Using tongs, carefully remove the cups and allow them to cool slightly. Remove the beans and place the cups to the side. In a bowl, whisk together the chili, soy sauce, sesame oil, and sriracha. Toss in tuna, cucumber, avocado, and scallions. Place 2 heaping tbsp of the tuna mixture into each wonton cup. Top with sesame seeds and serve immediately.

Variations & Ingredients Tips:

- Use salmon, shrimp or tofu instead of tuna for different proteins.
- Add some shredded carrots, cabbage or edamame to the vegetable mix.
- Drizzle with wasabi mayo, ponzu sauce or unagi sauce before serving.

Per Serving: Calories: 243; Total Fat: 9g; Saturated Fat: 2g; Cholesterol: 26mg; Sodium: 654mg; Total Carbs: 21g; Dietary Fiber: 3g; Total Sugars: 2g; Protein: 20g

Beet Chips

Servings: 4 | Prep Time: 10 Minutes | Cooking Time: 20 Minutes

Ingredients:

- 2 large red beets, washed and skinned
- 1 tablespoon avocado oil
- ¼ teaspoon salt

Directions:

1. Preheat the air fryer to 165°C/330°F.
2. Using a mandolin or sharp knife, slice the beets in 3 mm slices. Place them in a bowl of water and let them soak for 30 minutes. Drain the water and pat the beets dry with a paper towel or kitchen cloth.
3. In a medium bowl, toss the beets with avocado oil and sprinkle them with salt.
4. Lightly spray the air fryer basket with olive oil mist and place the beet chips into the basket. To allow for even

cooking, don't overlap the beets; cook in batches if necessary.

5. Cook the beet chips 15 to 20 minutes, shaking the basket every 5 minutes, until the outer edges of the beets begin to flip up like a chip. Remove from the basket and serve warm. Repeat with the remaining chips until they're all cooked.

Variations & Ingredients Tips:

- Use golden beets for a milder flavor and pretty color.
- Season with garlic powder, smoked paprika or herbs de Provence.
- Serve with hummus, guacamole or tzatziki for dipping.

Per Serving: Calories: 76; Total Fat: 4g; Saturated Fat: 1g; Cholesterol: 0mg; Sodium: 165mg; Total Carbs: 10g; Dietary Fiber: 2g; Total Sugars: 7g; Protein: 2g

Garlic Breadsticks

Servings: 12 | Prep Time: 10 Minutes | Cooking Time: 7 Minutes

Ingredients:

- 1½ tablespoons Olive oil
- 1½ teaspoons Minced garlic
- ¼ teaspoon Table salt
- ¼ teaspoon Ground black pepper
- 170 g Purchased pizza dough (vegan dough, if that's a concern)

Directions:

1. Preheat the air fryer to 200°C/400°F. Mix the oil, garlic, salt, and pepper in a small bowl.
2. Divide the pizza dough into 4 balls for a small air fryer, 6 for a medium machine, or 8 for a large, each ball about the size of a walnut in its shell. (Each should weigh 30 g, if you want to drag out a scale and get obsessive.) Roll each ball into a 13 cm long stick under your clean palms on a clean, dry work surface. Brush the sticks with the oil mixture.
3. When the machine is at temperature, place the prepared dough sticks in the basket, leaving a 2.5 cm space between them. Air-fry undisturbed for 7 minutes, or until puffed, golden, and set to the touch.
4. Use kitchen tongs to gently transfer the breadsticks to a wire rack and repeat step 3 with the remaining dough sticks.

Variations & Ingredients Tips:

- Sprinkle the breadsticks with grated Parmesan, sesame seeds or everything bagel seasoning before cooking.
- Serve with marinara sauce, garlic butter or ranch dressing for dipping.
- Make a sweet version by brushing with cinnamon-sugar butter instead of garlic oil.

Per Serving: Calories: 58; Total Fat: 3g; Saturated Fat: 0g; Cholesterol: 0mg; Sodium: 105mg; Total Carbs: 7g; Dietary Fiber: 0g; Total Sugars: 0g; Protein: 1g

Okra Chips

Servings: 4 | Prep Time: 10 Minutes | Cooking Time: 16 Minutes

Ingredients:

- 565 g thin fresh okra pods, cut into 2.5-cm pieces
- 1½ tbsp vegetable or canola oil
- ¾ tsp coarse sea salt or kosher salt

Directions:

1. Preheat the air fryer to 200°C/400°F. Toss the okra, oil, and salt in a large bowl until the pieces are well and evenly coated. When the machine is at temperature, pour the contents of the bowl into the basket. Air-fry, tossing several times, for 16 minutes, or until crisp and quite brown (maybe even a little blackened on the thin bits). Pour the contents of the basket onto a wire rack. Cool for a couple of minutes before serving.

Variations & Ingredients Tips:

- Sprinkle with paprika, chili powder, or garlic powder for extra flavor.
- Serve with ranch dressing or aioli for dipping.
- Use this method with other vegetables like zucchini, eggplant, or green beans.

Per Serving: Calories: 101; Total Fat: 7g; Saturated Fat: 1g; Cholesterol: no data; Sodium: 415mg; Total Carbs: 9g; Dietary Fiber: 4g; Total Sugars: 2g; Protein: 2g

Buffalo Wings

Servings: 2 | Prep Time: 10 Minutes (plus 2 Hours Marinating Time) | Cooking Time: 12 Minutes Per Batch

Ingredients:

- 900-g chicken wings
- 3 tablespoons butter, melted
- ¼ cup hot sauce
- Finishing Sauce:
- 3 tablespoons butter, melted
- ¼ cup hot sauce
- 1 teaspoon Worcestershire sauce

Directions:

1. Prepare the chicken wings by cutting off the wing tips and discarding (or freezing for chicken stock). Divide the drumettes from the wingettes by cutting through the joint. Place the chicken wing pieces in a large bowl.

2. Combine the melted butter and the hot sauce and stir to blend well. Pour the marinade over the chicken wings, cover and let the wings marinate for 2 hours or up to overnight in the refrigerator.
3. Preheat the air fryer to 200°C/400°F.
4. Air-fry the wings in two batches for 10 minutes per batch, shaking the basket halfway through the cooking process. When both batches are done, toss all the wings back into the basket for another 2 minutes to heat through and finish cooking.
5. While the wings are air-frying, combine the remaining 3 tbsp of butter, 60ml of hot sauce and the Worcestershire sauce. Remove the wings from the air fryer, toss them in the finishing sauce and serve with some cooling blue cheese dip and celery sticks.

Variations & Ingredients Tips:

- Adjust the amount of hot sauce to make the wings milder or spicier.
- Use a different hot sauce like sriracha or gochujang for an Asian twist.
- Sprinkle the wings with garlic powder, onion powder, or smoked paprika before air frying for extra flavor.

Per Serving: Calories: 620; Total Fat: 50g; Saturated Fat: 24g; Cholesterol: 220mg; Sodium: 1780mg; Total Carbohydrates: 2g; Dietary Fiber: 0g; Total Sugars: 0g; Protein: 41g

Cheddar Stuffed Jalapeños

Servings: 5 | Prep Time: 10 Minutes | Cooking Time: 15 Minutes

Ingredients:

- 10 jalapeño peppers
- 170 g ricotta cheese
- ¼ cup grated cheddar
- 2 tbsp bread crumbs

Directions:

1. Preheat air fryer to 170°C/340°F. Cut jalapeños in half lengthwise. Clean out the seeds and membrane. Set aside. Microwave ricotta cheese in a small bowl for 15 seconds to soften. Stir in cheddar cheese to combine. Stuff each jalapeño half with the cheese mixture. Top the poppers with bread crumbs. Place in air fryer and lightly spray with cooking oil. Bake for 5-6 minutes. Serve warm.

Variations & Ingredients Tips:

- Add some cooked bacon bits or chorizo to the cheese filling.
- Top with a slice of pepper jack cheese before air frying.
- Serve with ranch or queso dip for dunking.

Per Serving: Calories: 156; Total Fat: 10g; Saturated Fat: 6g; Cholesterol: 38mg; Sodium: 204mg; Total Carbs: 7g; Dietary Fiber: 1g; Total Sugars: 2g; Protein: 10g

Wrapped Shrimp Bites

Servings: 4 | Prep Time: 5 Minutes | Cooking Time: 15 Minutes

Ingredients:

- 2 jumbo shrimp, peeled
- 2 bacon strips, sliced
- 2 tbsp lemon juice
- ½ tsp chipotle powder
- ½ tsp garlic salt

Directions:

1. Preheat air fryer to 175°C/350°F. Wrap the bacon around the shrimp and place the shrimp in the foil-lined frying basket, seam side down. Drizzle with lemon juice, chipotle powder and garlic salt. Air fry for 10 minutes, turning the shrimp once until cooked through and bacon is crispy. Serve hot.

Variations & Ingredients Tips:

- Use prosciutto, pancetta, or turkey bacon instead of regular bacon for a different flavor.
- Brush the wrapped shrimp with BBQ sauce, teriyaki sauce, or pesto before cooking for extra seasoning.
- Serve with cocktail sauce, remoulade, or mango salsa for dipping.

Per Serving: Calories: 59; Total Fat: 3g; Saturated Fat: 1g; Cholesterol: 55mg; Sodium: 619mg; Total Carbohydrates: 1g; Dietary Fiber: 0g; Total Sugars: 0g; Protein: 7g

Crispy Okra Fries

Servings: 4 | Prep Time: 15 Minutes | Cooking Time: 25 Minutes

Ingredients:

- 225 g trimmed okra, cut lengthways
- ¼ tsp deggi mirch chili powder
- 3 tbsp buttermilk
- 2 tbsp chickpea flour
- 2 tbsp cornmeal
- Salt and pepper to taste

Directions:

1. Preheat air fryer to 190°C/380°F. Set out 2 bowls. In one, add buttermilk. In the second, mix flour, cornmeal, chili powder, salt, and pepper. Dip the okra in buttermilk, then dredge in flour and cornmeal. Transfer to the frying basket and spray the okra with oil. Air Fry for 10 minutes, shaking once halfway through cooking until crispy. Let cool for a few minutes and serve warm.

Variations & Ingredients Tips:

- Use zucchini, green beans or asparagus instead of okra.
- Add some garam masala, curry powder or cumin to the breading.
- Serve with mint-yogurt chutney or sriracha mayo for

dipping.

Per Serving: Calories: 93; Total Fat: 2g; Saturated Fat: 0g; Cholesterol: 2mg; Sodium: 37mg; Total Carbs: 16g; Dietary Fiber: 3g; Total Sugars: 3g; Protein: 4g

Five Spice Fries

Servings: 2 | Prep Time: 10 Minutes | Cooking Time: 30 Minutes

Ingredients:

- 1 Yukon Gold potato, cut into fries
- 1 tbsp coconut oil
- 1 tsp coconut sugar
- 1 tsp garlic powder
- ½ tsp Chinese five-spice
- Salt to taste
- ¼ tsp turmeric
- ¼ tsp paprika

Directions:

1. Preheat air fryer to 200°C/390°F. Toss the potato pieces with coconut oil, sugar, garlic, Chinese five-spice, salt, turmeric, and paprika in a bowl and stir well. Place in the greased frying basket and Air Fry for 18-25 minutes, tossing twice until softened and golden. Serve warm.

Variations & Ingredients Tips:

- Use sweet potatoes or parsnips instead of Yukon Gold.
- Add some cumin, coriander or garam masala for an Indian flavor.
- Serve with curry ketchup or mango chutney for dipping.

Per Serving: Calories: 164; Total Fat: 7g; Saturated Fat: 6g; Cholesterol: 0mg; Sodium: 299mg; Total Carbs: 24g; Dietary Fiber: 2g; Total Sugars: 3g; Protein: 2g

Prosciutto Mozzarella Bites

Servings: 8 | Prep Time: 10 Minutes | Cooking Time: 6 Minutes

Ingredients:

- 8 pieces full-fat mozzarella string cheese
- 8 thin slices prosciutto
- 16 basil leaves

Directions:

1. Preheat the air fryer to 180°C/360°F. Cut the string cheese in half across the center, not lengthwise. Do the same with the prosciutto. Place a piece of prosciutto onto a clean workspace. Top the prosciutto with a basil leaf and then a piece of string cheese. Roll up the string cheese inside the prosciutto and secure with a wooden toothpick. Repeat with the remaining cheese sticks. Place the prosciutto mozzarella bites into the air fryer basket and cook for 6 minutes, checking for doneness at 4 minutes.

Variations & Ingredients Tips:

- Use sliced salami, sopressata, or coppa instead of prosciutto for a different flavor.
- Wrap the cheese sticks with strips of roasted red peppers or sun-dried tomatoes for added color and tang.
- Drizzle with balsamic glaze or pesto before serving for an extra pop of flavor.

Per Serving: Calories: 94; Total Fat: 6g; Saturated Fat: 3g; Cholesterol: 24mg; Sodium: 382mg; Total Carbs: 0g; Dietary Fiber: 0g; Total Sugars: 0g; Protein: 9g

Cinnamon Sweet Potato Fries

Servings: 5 | Prep Time: 10 Minutes | Cooking Time: 30 Minutes

Ingredients:

- 3 sweet potatoes
- 2 tsp butter, melted
- 1 tsp cinnamon
- Salt and pepper to taste

Directions:

1. Preheat air fryer to 200°C/400°F. Peel the potatoes and slice them thinly crosswise. Transfer the slices to a large bowl. Toss with butter, cinnamon, salt, and pepper until fully coated. Place half of the slices into the air fryer. Stacking is ok. Air Fry for 10 minutes. Shake the basket, and cook for another 10 -12 minutes until crispy. Serve hot.

Variations & Ingredients Tips:

- Sprinkle the fries with brown sugar or maple syrup after cooking.
- Use pumpkin pie spice or apple pie spice instead of cinnamon.
- Serve with marshmallow fluff or caramel sauce for dipping.

Per Serving: Calories: 123; Total Fat: 3g; Saturated Fat: 2g; Cholesterol: 5mg; Sodium: 112mg; Total Carbs: 24g; Dietary Fiber: 3g; Total Sugars: 6g; Protein: 2g

Vegetable Side Dishes Recipes

Gorgonzola Stuffed Mushrooms

Servings: 2 | Prep Time: 10 Minutes | Cooking Time: 15 Minutes

Ingredients:

- 12 white button mushroom caps
- 2 tbsp diced white button mushroom stems
- 1/4 cup Gorgonzola cheese, crumbled
- 1 tsp olive oil
- 1 green onion, chopped
- 2 tbsp bread crumbs

Directions:

1. Preheat air fryer to 180°C/350°F.
2. Rub around the top of each mushroom cap with olive oil.
3. Mix the mushroom stems, green onion, and Gorgonzola cheese in a bowl.
4. Distribute and press mixture into the cups of mushrooms, then sprinkle bread crumbs on top.
5. Place stuffed mushrooms in the frying basket and bake for 5-7 minutes.
6. Serve right away.

Variations & Ingredients Tips:

- Use different cheese varieties like feta or blue cheese.
- Add chopped spinach or artichokes to the filling.
- Sprinkle with parmesan before baking.

Per Serving: Calories: 150; Total Fat: 9g; Saturated Fat: 4.5g; Cholesterol: 20mg; Sodium: 320mg; Total Carbohydrates: 10g; Dietary Fiber: 2g; Total Sugars: 3g; Protein: 8g

Smoked Avocado Wedges

Servings: 4 | Prep Time: 5 Minutes | Cooking Time: 15 Minutes

Ingredients:

- ½ teaspoon smoked paprika
- 2 teaspoons olive oil
- ½ lime, juiced
- 8 peeled avocado wedges
- 1 teaspoon chipotle powder
- ¼ teaspoon salt

Directions:

1. Preheat air fryer to 200°C/400°F.
2. Drizzle the avocado wedges with olive oil and lime juice.
3. In a bowl, combine chipotle powder, smoked paprika, and salt. Sprinkle over the avocado wedges.
4. Place them in the frying basket and Air Fry for 7 minutes.
5. Serve immediately.

Variations & Ingredients Tips:

- Use lemon juice instead of lime juice for a different citrus flavor.
- Add some chopped cilantro or parsley for a fresh herb flavor.
- Serve the avocado wedges with salsa or guacamole for a Mexican-inspired side dish.

Per Serving: Calories: 130; Total Fat: 12g; Saturated Fat: 1.5g; Cholesterol: 0mg; Sodium: 150mg; Total Carbs: 6g; Fiber: 5g; Sugars: 0g; Protein: 1g

Buttered Brussels Sprouts

Servings: 4 | Prep Time: 5 Minutes | Cooking Time: 30 Minutes

Ingredients:

- ¼ cup grated Parmesan
- 2 tbsp butter, melted
- 455g Brussels sprouts
- Salt and pepper to taste

Directions:

1. Preheat air fryer to 165°C/330°F.
2. Trim the bottoms of the sprouts and remove any discolored leaves.
3. Place the sprouts in a medium bowl along with butter, salt and pepper. Toss to coat, then place them in the frying basket.
4. Roast for 20 minutes, shaking the basket twice. When done, the sprouts should be crisp with golden-brown color.
5. Plate the sprouts in a serving dish and toss with Parmesan cheese.

Variations & Ingredients Tips:

- Add crushed garlic or garlic powder to the butter mixture.
- Toss with balsamic glaze or lemon juice after cooking.
- Use olive oil instead of butter to make it vegan.

Per Serving: Calories: 130; Total Fat: 8g; Saturated Fat: 4g; Cholesterol: 15mg; Sodium: 230mg; Total Carbs: 11g; Fiber: 4g; Sugars: 3g; Protein: 6g

Mashed Potato Tots

Servings: 18 | Prep Time: 20 Minutes | Cooking

Time: 10 Minutes

Ingredients:

- 1 medium potato or 1 cup cooked mashed potatoes
- 1 tablespoon real bacon bits
- 2 tablespoons chopped green onions, tops only
- 1/4 teaspoon onion powder
- 1 teaspoon dried chopped chives
- Salt
- 2 tablespoons flour
- 1 egg white, beaten
- 1/2 cup panko breadcrumbs
- Oil for misting or cooking spray

Directions:

1. If using cooked mashed potatoes, jump to step 4.
2. Boil potato until tender, about 10 mins. Drain, cool in ice water, then drain again and mash.
3. Preheat air fryer to 200°C/390°F.
4. In a bowl, mix potatoes, bacon bits, onions, onion powder, chives, salt, and flour.
5. Stir in egg white.
6. Place panko crumbs on wax paper.
7. Scoop 2 tsp potato mixture, roll in panko to coat.
8. Mist tots with oil and place in single layer in air fryer basket.
9. Cook at 200°C/390°F for 10 mins until browned and crispy.
10. Repeat with remaining tots.

Variations & Ingredients Tips:

- Stir shredded cheddar into potato mixture.
- Use seasoned breadcrumbs instead of panko.
- Serve with ranch, sour cream or cheese sauce for dipping.

Per Serving (3 tots): Calories: 42; Total Fat: 0.6g; Saturated Fat: 0.1g; Cholesterol: 0mg; Sodium: 27mg; Total Carbs: 7g; Dietary Fiber: 0.4g; Total Sugars: 0.3g; Protein: 1g

Dilly Sesame Roasted Asparagus

Servings: 6 | Prep Time: 5 Minutes | Cooking Time: 15 Minutes

Ingredients:

- 454g asparagus, trimmed
- 1 tbsp butter, melted
- ¼ tsp salt
- 1 clove garlic, minced
- 2 tsp chopped dill
- 3 tbsp sesame seeds

Directions:

1. Preheat air fryer to 188°C/370°F.
2. Combine asparagus and butter in a bowl.
3. Place asparagus mixture in the frying basket and Roast for 9 minutes, tossing once.
4. Transfer it to a serving dish and stir in salt, garlic, sesame seeds and dill until coated.
5. Serve immediately.

Variations & Ingredients Tips:

- Use olive oil instead of butter.
- Add lemon zest or red pepper flakes for extra zing.
- Substitute parsley or chives for the dill.

Per Serving: Calories: 75; Total Fat: 5g; Saturated Fat: 2g; Cholesterol: 7mg; Sodium: 95mg; Total Carbs: 5g; Fiber: 2g; Sugars: 2g; Protein: 3g

Tuna Platter

Servings: 4 | Prep Time: 20 Minutes | Cooking Time: 9 Minutes

Ingredients:

- 4 new potatoes, boiled in their jackets
- ½ cup vinaigrette dressing, plus 2 tablespoons
- 225 g fresh green beans, cut in 1.3-cm pieces and steamed
- 1 tbsp Herbes de Provence
- 1 tbsp minced shallots
- 1½ tbsp tarragon vinegar
- 4 tuna steaks, each 2-cm thick, about 450 g
- salt and pepper
- Salad
- 8 cups chopped romaine lettuce
- 12 grape tomatoes, halved lengthwise
- ½ cup pitted olives (black, green, nicoise, or combination)
- 2 boiled eggs, peeled and halved lengthwise

Directions:

1. Quarter potatoes and toss with 1 tablespoon salad dressing. Toss the warm beans with the other tablespoon of salad dressing. Set both aside while you prepare the tuna. Mix together the herbs, shallots, and vinegar and rub into all sides of tuna. Season fish to taste with salt and pepper. Cook tuna at 200°C/390°F for 7 minutes and check. If needed, cook 2 minutes longer, until tuna is barely pink in the center. Spread the lettuce over a large platter. Slice the tuna steaks in 3-cm pieces and arrange them in the center of the lettuce. Place the remaining ingredients around the tuna. Diners create their own plates by selecting what they want from the platter. Pass remainder of salad dressing at the table.

Variations & Ingredients Tips:

- Use salmon, swordfish, or mahi-mahi instead of tuna for a different fish option.
- Add marinated artichoke hearts, roasted red peppers, or capers to the platter for extra Mediterranean flavors.
- Serve with a lemon wedge and crusty bread on the side.

Per Serving: Calories: 470; Total Fat: 23g; Saturated Fat: 4g; Cholesterol: 157mg; Sodium: 621mg; Total Carbohydrates: 25g; Dietary Fiber: 6g; Total Sugars: 5g; Protein: 42g

Simple Baked Potatoes With Dill Yogurt

Servings: 4 | Prep Time: 5 Minutes | Cooking Time: 45 Minutes

Ingredients:

- 4 Yukon gold potatoes
- Salt and black pepper
- Cooking oil spray
- 1/2 cup Greek yogurt
- 1/4 cup minced fresh dill

Directions:

1. Pierce potatoes several times with a fork. Lightly coat with cooking spray and season with salt.
2. Preheat air fryer to 205°C/400°F.
3. Place potatoes in greased air fryer basket.
4. Air fry for 30-35 minutes, flipping halfway, until potatoes are cooked through and slightly crispy.
5. Transfer baked potatoes to a serving dish.
6. Top each potato with a dollop of Greek yogurt and sprinkle with minced dill, salt and pepper.

Variations & Ingredients Tips:

- Use russet or sweet potatoes instead of Yukon gold.
- Add garlic, chives or bacon bits to the yogurt topping.
- Brush potatoes with olive oil or melted butter before baking.

Per Serving: Calories: 165; Total Fat: 1g; Saturated Fat: 0g; Cholesterol: 2mg; Sodium: 106mg; Total Carbs: 34g; Dietary Fiber: 3g; Total Sugars: 3g; Protein: 6g

Almond-crusted Zucchini Fries

Servings: 2 | Prep Time: 15 Minutes | Cooking Time: 30 Minutes

Ingredients:

- ½ cup grated Pecorino cheese
- 1 zucchini, cut into fries
- 1 tsp salt
- 1 egg
- 1 tbsp almond milk
- ½ cup almond flour

Directions:

1. Preheat air fryer to 188°C/370°F. Distribute zucchini fries evenly over a paper towel, sprinkle with salt, and let sit for 10 minutes to pull out moisture. Pat them dry with paper towels.
2. In a bowl, beat egg and almond milk. In another bowl, combine almond flour and Pecorino cheese.
3. Dip fries in egg mixture and then dredge them in flour mixture.
4. Place zucchini fries in the lightly greased frying basket and Air Fry for 10 minutes, flipping once. Serve.

Variations & Ingredients Tips:

- Use gluten-free breadcrumbs instead of almond flour.
- Add dried herbs or spices to the coating for extra flavor.
- Serve with marinara sauce for dipping.

Per Serving: Calories: 272; Total Fat: 18g; Saturated Fat: 5g; Cholesterol: 116mg; Sodium: 1070mg; Total Carbs: 16g; Fiber: 4g; Sugars: 5g; Protein: 15g

Perfect Asparagus

Servings: 3 | Prep Time: 5 Minutes | Cooking Time: 10 Minutes

Ingredients:

- 454g very thin asparagus spears
- 2 tablespoons olive oil
- 1 teaspoon coarse sea salt or kosher salt
- 3/4 teaspoon finely grated lemon zest

Directions:

1. Preheat the air fryer to 205°C/400°F.
2. Trim bottoms of asparagus to fit basket. Arrange on a plate and drizzle with olive oil, turning to coat all spears.
3. When machine is at temperature, place spears in basket. They may touch.
4. Air fry for 10 minutes, tossing and rearranging twice, until tender.
5. Transfer to a serving platter. Sprinkle with salt and lemon zest while warm.
6. Serve immediately.

Variations & Ingredients Tips:

- Use thicker asparagus spears and increase cooking time slightly.
- Drizzle with balsamic glaze or melted butter before serving.
- Top with grated parmesan cheese or toasted almonds.

Per Serving: Calories: 81; Total Fat: 7g; Saturated Fat: 1g; Cholesterol: 0mg; Sodium: 394mg; Total Carbohydrates: 4g; Dietary Fiber: 2g; Total Sugars: 2g; Protein: 2g

Fried Corn On The Cob

Servings: 2 | Prep Time: 10 Minutes | Cooking Time: 10 Minutes

Ingredients:

- 1½ tablespoons Regular or low-fat mayonnaise
- 1½ teaspoons Minced garlic
- ¼ teaspoon Table salt
- ¾ cup Plain panko bread crumbs
- 3 10cm lengths husked and de-silked corn on the cob
- Vegetable oil spray

Directions:

1. Preheat air fryer to 200°C/400°F.
2. Stir mayo, garlic, salt. Spread panko on a plate.
3. Brush mayo mix over corn kernels. Roll in panko to coat.
4. Spray corn with oil. Set aside and coat remaining pieces.
5. Set coated corn in basket with space between. Air fry 10 mins until crisp.
6. Transfer to wire rack. Cool 5 mins before serving.

Variations & Ingredients Tips:

- Use chipotle mayo for a smoky flavor.
- Add parmesan or cajun seasoning to the breadcrumb coating.
- Serve with lime wedges for squeezing over.

Per Serving: Calories: 210; Total Fat: 8g; Saturated Fat: 1g; Cholesterol: 5mg; Sodium: 440mg; Total Carbs: 31g; Fiber: 3g; Sugars: 3g; Protein: 6g

Veggie Fritters

Servings: 4 | Prep Time: 15 Minutes | Cooking Time: 35 Minutes

Ingredients:

- ¼ cup crumbled feta cheese
- 1 grated zucchini
- ¼ cup Parmesan cheese
- 2 tbsp minced onion
- 1 tbsp garlic powder
- 1 tbsp flour
- 1 tbsp cornmeal
- 1 tbsp butter, melted
- 1 egg
- 2 tsp chopped dill
- 2 tsp chopped parsley
- Salt and pepper to taste
- 1 cup bread crumbs

Directions:

1. Preheat air fryer at 175°C/350°F. Squeeze grated zucchini between paper towels to remove excess moisture. In a bowl, combine all ingredients except breadcrumbs. Form mixture into 12 balls, about 2 tbsp each. In a shallow bowl, add breadcrumbs. Roll each ball in breadcrumbs, covering all sides. Place fritters on an ungreased pizza pan. Place in the frying basket and air fry for 11 minutes, flipping once. Serve.

Variations & Ingredients Tips:

- Add grated carrots, sweet potatoes, or beets for a colorful twist.
- Use goat cheese, ricotta, or mozzarella instead of feta for a different flavor profile.
- Serve with tzatziki sauce, marinara sauce, or ranch dressing for dipping.

Per Serving: Calories: 264; Total Fat: 14g; Saturated Fat: 7g; Cholesterol: 74mg; Sodium: 566mg; Total Carbohydrates: 25g; Dietary Fiber: 2g; Total Sugars: 3g; Protein: 11g

Rich Spinach Chips

Servings: 4 | Prep Time: 5 Minutes | Cooking Time: 20 Minutes

Ingredients:

- 284g spinach
- 2 tbsp lemon juice
- 2 tbsp olive oil
- Salt and pepper to taste
- 1/2 tsp garlic powder
- 1/2 tsp onion powder

Directions:

1. Preheat air fryer to 177°C/350°F.
2. Place spinach in a bowl and drizzle with lemon juice and olive oil. Massage with your hands.
3. Season spinach with salt, pepper, garlic powder and onion powder. Toss gently to coat.
4. Arrange spinach in a single layer in the air fryer basket.
5. Bake for 3 minutes, shake basket and bake 1-3 minutes more until crispy.
6. Let cool completely before serving.

Variations & Ingredients Tips:

- Use kale, beet greens or chard instead of spinach.
- Add parmesan, nutritional yeast or ranch seasoning before baking.
- Bake at a lower temp for chewier chips.

Per Serving: Calories: 61; Total Fat: 5g; Saturated Fat: 1g; Cholesterol: 0mg; Sodium: 46mg; Total Carbohydrates: 4g; Dietary Fiber: 3g; Total Sugars: 1g; Protein: 2g

Asparagus Fries

Servings: 4 | Prep Time: 10 Minutes | Cooking Time: 5 Minutes Per Batch

Ingredients:

- 340g fresh asparagus spears with tough ends trimmed off
- 2 egg whites
- ¼ cup water
- ¾ cup panko breadcrumbs
- ¼ cup grated Parmesan cheese, plus 2 tablespoons
- ¼ teaspoon salt
- Oil for misting or cooking spray

Directions:

1. Preheat air fryer to 199°C/390°F.
2. In a shallow dish, beat egg whites and water until slightly foamy.
3. In another shallow dish, combine panko, Parmesan, and salt.
4. Dip asparagus spears in egg, then roll in crumbs. Spray with oil or cooking spray.
5. Place a layer of asparagus in air fryer basket, leaving just

a little space in between each spear. Stack another layer on top, crosswise. Cook at 199°C/390°F for 5 minutes, until crispy and golden brown.

6. Repeat to cook remaining asparagus.

Variations & Ingredients Tips:

- Use gluten-free breadcrumbs instead of panko.
- Add grated parmesan or ranch seasoning to the coating.
- Serve with a dip like ranch, marinara or cheese sauce.

Per Serving: Calories: 120; Total Fat: 3g; Saturated Fat: 1g; Cholesterol: 6mg; Sodium: 310mg; Total Carbs: 16g; Fiber: 2g; Sugars: 2g; Protein: 7g

Cheese-rice Stuffed Bell Peppers

Servings: 4 | Prep Time: 15 Minutes | Cooking Time: 30 Minutes

Ingredients:

- 2 red bell peppers, halved and seeds and stem removed
- 1 cup cooked brown rice
- 2 tomatoes, diced
- 1 garlic clove, minced
- Salt and pepper to taste
- 113g goat cheese
- 3 tbsp basil, chopped
- 3 tbsp oregano, chopped
- 1 tbsp parsley, chopped
- ¼ cup grated Parmesan

Directions:

1. Preheat air fryer to 182°C/360°F.
2. Place the brown rice, tomatoes, garlic, salt, and pepper in a bowl and stir.
3. Divide the rice filling evenly among the bell pepper halves.
4. Combine the goat cheese, basil, parsley and oregano in a small bowl.
5. Sprinkle each bell pepper with the herbed cheese.
6. Arrange the bell peppers in the air fryer and Bake for 20 minutes.
7. Serve topped with grated Parmesan and parsley.

Variations & Ingredients Tips:

- Use quinoa or farro instead of brown rice.
- Stuff with a meat and veggie filling instead.
- Top with breadcrumbs before baking for a crunchy topping.

Per Serving: Calories: 250; Total Fat: 10g; Saturated Fat: 6g; Cholesterol: 20mg; Sodium: 290mg; Total Carbs: 29g; Fiber: 5g; Sugars: 8g; Protein: 12g

Pecorino Dill Muffins

Servings: 4 | Prep Time: 10 Minutes | Cooking Time: 25 Minutes

Ingredients:

- 1/4 cup grated Pecorino cheese
- 1 cup flour
- 1 tsp dried dill
- 1/8 tsp salt
- 1/4 tsp onion powder
- 2 tsp baking powder
- 1 egg
- 1/4 cup Greek yogurt

Directions:

1. Preheat air fryer to 180°C/350°F.
2. In a bowl, combine the dry ingredients (pecorino, flour, dill, salt, onion powder, baking powder).
3. In another bowl, whisk the wet ingredients (egg, yogurt).
4. Add wet to dry ingredients and stir until just combined.
5. Transfer batter to 6 greased silicone muffin cups.
6. Place muffin cups in air fryer basket and bake for 12 minutes.
7. Serve right away.

Variations & Ingredients Tips:

- Use cheddar or parmesan cheese instead of pecorino.
- Add chopped chives or green onions to the batter.
- Substitute milk or buttermilk for the Greek yogurt.

Per Serving: Calories: 153; Total Fat: 5g; Saturated Fat: 2g; Cholesterol: 36mg; Sodium: 301mg; Total Carbohydrates: 21g; Dietary Fiber: 1g; Total Sugars: 2g; Protein: 7g

Perfect French Fries

Servings: 3 | Prep Time: 10 Minutes | Cooking Time: 37 Minutes

Ingredients:

- 454g large russet potatoes
- Vegetable oil or olive oil spray
- 1/2 teaspoon table salt

Directions:

1. Cut each potato lengthwise into 6mm thick slices, then cut each slice into 6mm thick fry strips.
2. Soak the fry strips in cool water for 5 minutes. Drain and pat very dry with paper towels.
3. Preheat air fryer to 110°C/225°F.
4. Arrange fries in an even layer in the basket and air fry for 20 minutes, tossing twice.
5. Transfer fries to a bowl. Increase air fryer temperature to 160°C/325°F.
6. Generously coat fries with oil spray, tossing several times to evenly coat all over.
7. When air fryer is at temp, return fries to basket and air fry 12 minutes, tossing twice.
8. Increase temperature to 190°C/375°F. Air fry 5 more minutes, tossing frequently, until browned and crispy.
9. Transfer to a bowl, toss with salt, and serve hot.

Variations & Ingredients Tips:

- Cut fries into thin shoestring or thicker steak fry shapes.
- Toss with cajun seasoning, ranch powder or grated parmesan.
- Serve with ketchup, ranch, cheese sauce or chili for dipping/topping.

Per Serving: Calories: 189; Total Fat: 0g; Saturated Fat: 0g; Cholesterol: 0mg; Sodium: 147mg; Total Carbohydrates: 42g; Dietary Fiber: 3g; Total Sugars: 2g; Protein: 4g

Mediterranean Roasted Vegetables

Servings: 4 | Prep Time: 10 Minutes | Cooking Time: 30 Minutes

Ingredients:

- 1 red bell pepper, cut into chunks
- 1 cup sliced mushrooms
- 1 cup green beans, diced
- 1 zucchini, sliced
- 1/3 cup diced red onion
- 3 garlic cloves, sliced
- 2 tbsp olive oil
- 1 tsp rosemary
- 1/2 tsp flaked sea salt

Directions:

1. Preheat air fryer to 180°C/350°F.
2. Add the bell pepper, mushrooms, green beans, red onion, zucchini, rosemary, and garlic to a bowl and mix.
3. Spritz with olive oil and stir until well-coated.
4. Put the veggies in the frying basket and air fry for 14-18 minutes until crispy and softened.
5. Serve sprinkled with flaked sea salt.

Variations & Ingredients Tips:

- Add diced eggplant or cherry tomatoes.
- Use balsamic vinegar instead of olive oil.
- Toss with fresh basil or parmesan after cooking.

Per Serving: Calories: 88; Total Fat: 5g; Saturated Fat: 1g; Cholesterol: 0mg; Sodium: 106mg; Total Carbohydrates: 10g; Dietary Fiber: 3g; Total Sugars: 5g; Protein: 3g

Mushrooms

Servings: 4 | Prep Time: 10 Minutes | Cooking Time: 12 Minutes

Ingredients:

- 227g whole white button mushrooms
- 1/2 teaspoon salt
- 1/8 teaspoon pepper
- 1/4 teaspoon garlic powder
- 1/4 teaspoon onion powder
- 5 tablespoons potato starch
- 1 egg, beaten
- 3/4 cup panko breadcrumbs
- Oil for misting or cooking spray

Directions:

1. Place mushrooms in a bowl. Add salt, pepper, garlic and onion powders and stir to coat.
2. Add potato starch and toss mushrooms until well coated.
3. Dip mushrooms in beaten egg, then roll in panko crumbs. Mist with oil spray.
4. Place mushrooms in air fryer basket. Stack them if needed.
5. Cook at 199°C/390°F for 5 minutes. Shake basket, then cook 7 more minutes until crispy.

Variations & Ingredients Tips:

- Use breadcrumbs instead of panko for a different texture.
- Add parmesan or ranch seasoning to the breading.
- Serve with ranch, blue cheese or marinara for dipping.

Per Serving: Calories: 138; Total Fat: 2g; Saturated Fat: 1g; Cholesterol: 47mg; Sodium: 524mg; Total Carbohydrates: 26g; Dietary Fiber: 2g; Total Sugars: 1g; Protein: 5g

Horseradish Potato Mash

Servings: 4 | Prep Time: 10 Minutes | Cooking Time: 50 Minutes

Ingredients:

- 454g baby potatoes
- 1 tbsp horseradish sauce
- 1/2 cup vegetable broth
- 1/2 tsp sea salt
- 3 tbsp butter
- 2 garlic cloves, minced
- 2 tsp chili powder

Directions:

1. Preheat the air fryer to 205°C/400°F.
2. Combine the potatoes, broth, and salt in a cake pan, then cover with foil and put in the frying basket. Bake for 20 minutes, stirring once until almost tender.
3. Drain and place potatoes on a baking sheet. With a glass bottom, smash the potatoes without breaking them apart.
4. In a saucepan, mix butter, garlic, chili powder, and horseradish sauce. Melt over low heat.
5. Brush butter mix over the smashed potatoes.
6. Place as many as will fit in the basket in a single layer, butter-side down. Brush tops with more butter mix.
7. Bake for 12-17 minutes, turning once until crisp. Keep cooked potatoes warm at 121°C/250°F while frying remaining batches.

Variations & Ingredients Tips:

- Add shredded cheese like cheddar to the butter mixture.
- Substitute sour cream for some of the butter.
- Top with chopped scallions or bacon bits.

Per Serving: Calories: 275; Total Fat: 14g; Saturated Fat: 8g; Cholesterol: 31mg; Sodium: 486mg; Total Carbs: 34g; Dietary Fiber: 3g; Total Sugars: 2g; Protein: 4g

Roasted Fennel Salad

Servings: 3 | Prep Time: 5 Minutes | Cooking Time: 20 Minutes

Ingredients:

- 3 cups (185g) trimmed and roughly chopped fennel
- 1 1/2 tablespoons olive oil
- 1/4 teaspoon table salt
- 1/4 teaspoon ground black pepper
- 1 1/2 tablespoons white balsamic vinegar

Directions:

1. Preheat air fryer to 204°C/400°F.
2. Toss the chopped fennel with olive oil, salt and pepper in a bowl until well coated.
3. Place fennel in air fryer basket, spreading into a single layer.
4. Air fry for 20 minutes, tossing and rearranging twice, until edges are golden and fennel is softened.
5. Transfer roasted fennel to a bowl and toss with the vinegar while hot.
6. Allow to cool slightly before serving warm or at room temperature.

Variations & Ingredients Tips:

- Add sliced shallots or garlic before roasting.
- Use apple cider or red wine vinegar instead of white balsamic.
- Top with toasted nuts or crumbled feta cheese.

Per Serving: Calories: 85; Total Fat: 6g; Saturated Fat: 1g; Cholesterol: 0mg; Sodium: 155mg; Total Carbohydrates: 7g; Dietary Fiber: 3g; Total Sugars: 2g; Protein: 1g

Poultry Recipes

Simple Salsa Chicken Thighs

Servings:2 | Prep Time: 5 Minutes | Cooking Time: 35 Minutes

Ingredients:

- 454 grams boneless, skinless chicken thighs
- 1 cup mild chunky salsa
- ½ tsp taco seasoning
- 2 lime wedges for serving

Directions:

1. Preheat air fryer to 180°C/350°F.
2. Add chicken thighs into a baking pan and pour salsa and taco seasoning over.
3. Place the pan in the air fryer basket and Air Fry for 30 minutes until golden brown.
4. Serve with lime wedges.

Variations & Ingredients Tips:

- Use spicy salsa or add diced jalapeños for a kick of heat.
- Sprinkle with shredded cheddar cheese during the last 5 minutes of cooking.
- Serve over rice, quinoa, or in tortillas for tacos.

Per Serving: Calories: 330; Total Fat: 11g; Saturated Fat: 3g; Sodium: 950mg; Total Carbohydrates: 10g; Dietary Fiber: 2g; Total Sugars: 6g; Protein: 45g

Chicken Burgers With Blue Cheese Sauce

Servings: 4 | Prep Time: 15 Minutes | Cooking Time: 40 Minutes

Ingredients:

- ¼ cup crumbled blue cheese
- ¼ cup sour cream
- 2 tbsp mayonnaise
- 1 tbsp red hot sauce
- Salt to taste
- 3 tbsp buffalo wing sauce
- 454 grams ground chicken
- 2 tbsp grated carrot
- 2 tbsp diced celery
- 1 egg white

Directions:

1. Whisk the blue cheese, sour cream, mayonnaise, red hot sauce, salt, and 1 tbsp of buffalo sauce in a bowl. Let sit covered in the fridge until ready to use.
2. Preheat air fryer at 180°C/350°F.
3. In another bowl, combine the remaining ingredients. Form mixture into 4 patties, making a slight indentation in the middle of each.
4. Place patties in the greased air fryer basket and Air Fry for 13 minutes until you reach your desired doneness, flipping once.
5. Serve with the blue cheese sauce.

Variations & Ingredients Tips:

- Use ground turkey or beef instead of chicken for different flavors.
- Add diced jalapeños or hot sauce to the patty mixture for extra heat.
- Serve on a bun with lettuce, tomato, and pickles for a complete burger.

Per Serving: Calories: 340; Total Fat: 24g; Saturated Fat: 8g; Sodium: 1080mg; Total Carbohydrates: 4g; Dietary Fiber: 0g; Total Sugars: 2g; Protein: 27g

Chicken Skewers

Servings: 4 | Prep Time: 20 Minutes | Cooking Time: 55 Minutes

Ingredients:

- 454 grams boneless skinless chicken thighs, cut into pieces
- 1 sweet onion, cut into 2.5-cm pieces
- 1 zucchini, cut into 2.5-cm pieces
- 1 red bell pepper, cut into 2.5-cm pieces
- ¼ cup olive oil
- 1 tsp garlic powder
- 1 tsp shallot powder
- 1 tsp ground cumin
- ½ tsp dried oregano
- ½ tsp dried thyme
- ¼ cup lemon juice
- 1 tbsp apple cider vinegar
- 12 grape tomatoes

Directions:

1. Combine the olive oil, garlic powder, shallot powder, cumin, oregano, thyme, lemon juice, and vinegar in a bowl; mix well. Alternate skewering the chicken, bell pepper, onion, zucchini, and tomatoes. Once all of the skewers are prepared, place them in a greased baking dish and pour the olive oil marinade over the top. Turn to coat. Cover with plastic wrap and refrigerate.
2. Preheat air fryer to 190°C/380°F.
3. Remove the skewers from the marinade and arrange them in a single layer on the air fryer basket. Bake for 25 minutes, rotating once. Let the skewers sit for 5 minutes.
4. Serve and enjoy!

Variations & Ingredients Tips:

- Use pork, beef, or shrimp instead of chicken for different protein options.
- Add mushrooms, eggplant, or yellow squash to the skewers for more veggies.
- Brush with BBQ sauce, teriyaki sauce, or pesto during the last few minutes of cooking.

Per Serving: Calories: 330; Total Fat: 20g; Saturated Fat: 3.5g; Sodium: 110mg; Total Carbohydrates: 9g; Dietary Fiber: 3g; Total Sugars: 5g; Protein: 29g

Chicken Wings Al Ajillo

Servings:4 | Prep Time: 10 Minutes | Cooking Time: 35 Minutes

Ingredients:

- 907 grams chicken wings, split at the joint
- 2 tbsp melted butter
- 2 tbsp grated Cotija cheese
- 4 cloves garlic, minced
- ½ tbsp hot paprika
- ¼ tsp salt

Directions:

1. Preheat air fryer to 120°C/250°F.
2. Coat the chicken wings with 1 tbsp of butter. Place them in the basket and Air Fry for 12 minutes, tossing once.
3. In another bowl, whisk 1 tbsp of butter, Cotija cheese, garlic, hot paprika, and salt. Reserve.
4. Increase temperature to 200°C/400°F. Air Fry wings for 10 more minutes, tossing twice.
5. Transfer them to the bowl with the sauce, and toss to coat.
6. Serve immediately.

Variations & Ingredients Tips:

- Use drumettes or whole wings instead of split wings.
- Substitute Cotija cheese with Parmesan, Pecorino Romano, or feta.
- Add a dash of cayenne pepper or red pepper flakes for extra heat.

Per Serving: Calories: 510; Total Fat: 41g; Saturated Fat: 15g; Sodium: 580mg; Total Carbohydrates: 2g; Dietary Fiber: 0g; Total Sugars: 0g; Protein: 35g

Turkey Burgers

Servings: 4 | Prep Time: 10 Minutes | Cooking Time: 13 Minutes

Ingredients:

- 450g ground turkey
- 1/4 cup diced red onion
- 1 tablespoon grilled chicken seasoning
- 1/2 teaspoon dried parsley
- 1/2 teaspoon salt
- 4 slices provolone cheese
- 4 whole-grain sandwich buns
- Suggested toppings: lettuce, sliced tomatoes, dill pickles, and mustard

Directions:

1. Combine turkey, onion, seasoning, parsley and salt. Mix well.
2. Shape into 4 patties.
3. Cook at 180°C/360°F for 11 mins until turkey is cooked through.
4. Top each burger with a cheese slice and cook 2 more mins

to melt.

5. Serve on buns with desired toppings.

Variations & Ingredients Tips:

- Use ground chicken instead of turkey.
- Add breadcrumbs or an egg to bind the patties if too wet.
- Top with avocado, sauteed mushrooms or caramelized onions.

Per Serving: Calories: 299; Total Fat: 10g; Saturated Fat: 4g; Cholesterol: 95mg; Sodium: 726mg; Total Carbs: 25g; Dietary Fiber: 3g; Total Sugars: 3g; Protein: 31g

Irresistible Cheesy Chicken Sticks

Servings: 2 | Prep Time: 20 Minutes | Cooking Time: 30 Minutes

Ingredients:

- 6 mozzarella sticks
- 1 cup flour
- 2 eggs, beaten
- 450g ground chicken
- 1 1/2 cups breadcrumbs
- 1/4 tsp crushed chilis
- 1/4 tsp cayenne pepper
- 1/2 tsp garlic powder
- 1/4 tsp shallot powder
- 1/2 tsp oregano

Directions:

1. Preheat air fryer to 200°C/390°F.
2. Combine crushed chilis, cayenne pepper, garlic powder, shallot powder, and oregano in a bowl. Add the ground chicken and mix well with your hands until evenly combined.
3. In another mixing bowl, beat the eggs until fluffy and until the yolks and whites are fully combined, and set aside.
4. Pour the beaten eggs, flour, and bread crumbs into 3 separate bowls.
5. Roll the mozzarella sticks in the flour, then dip them in the beaten eggs. With hands, wrap the stick in a thin layer of the chicken mixture. Finally, coat the sticks in the crumbs.
6. Place the sticks in the greased frying basket fryer and Air Fry for 18-20 minutes, turning once until crispy.
7. Serve hot.

Variations & Ingredients Tips:

- Use pepper Jack cheese sticks for extra spice.
- Substitute ground chicken with Italian sausage or chorizo.
- Serve with marinara or ranch for dipping.

Per Serving: Calories: 860; Total Fat: 35g; Saturated Fat: 13g; Cholesterol: 360mg; Sodium: 1380mg; Total Carbs: 74g; Dietary Fiber: 4g; Total Sugars: 5g; Protein: 63g

Chicken Pasta Pie

Servings: 4 | Prep Time: 20 Minutes | Cooking Time: 40 Minutes

Ingredients:

- 1/3 cup green bell peppers, diced
- 1/4 cup yellow bell peppers, diced
- 1/2 cup mozzarella cheese, grated
- 3/4 cup grated Parmesan cheese
- 2/3 cup ricotta cheese
- 2 tbsp butter, melted
- 1 egg
- 1/4 tsp salt
- 170g cooked spaghetti
- 2 tsp olive oil
- 1/3 cup diced onions
- 2 cloves minced garlic
- 115g ground chicken
- 1 cup marinara sauce
- 1/2 tsp dried oregano

Directions:

1. Combine the ricotta cheese, 1 tbsp of Parmesan cheese, minced garlic, and salt in a bowl.
2. Whisk the melted butter and egg in another bowl. Add the remaining Parmesan cheese and cooked spaghetti and mix well. Set aside.
3. Warm the olive oil in a skillet over medium heat. Add in onions, green bell peppers, yellow bell peppers and cook for 3 minutes until the onions tender.
4. Stir in ground chicken and cook for 5 minutes until no longer pink.
5. Preheat air fryer at 175°C/350°F.
6. Press spaghetti mixture into a greased baking pan, then spread ricotta mixture on top, and finally top with the topping mixture, followed by the marinara sauce.
7. Place baking pan in the frying basket and Bake for 10 minutes.
8. Scatter with mozzarella cheese on top and cook for 4 more minutes.
9. Let rest for 20 minutes before releasing the sides of the baking pan. Cut into slices and serve sprinkled with oregano.

Variations & Ingredients Tips:

- Use ground turkey instead of chicken.
- Add sauteed mushrooms or spinach to the filling.
- Substitute different cheese like cheddar or provolone.

Per Serving: Calories: 477; Total Fat: 23g; Saturated Fat: 11g; Cholesterol: 125mg; Sodium: 871mg; Total Carbs: 37g; Dietary Fiber: 3g; Total Sugars: 6g; Protein: 30g

Sage & Paprika Turkey Cutlets

Servings: 4 | Prep Time: 10 Minutes | Cooking Time: 15 Minutes

Ingredients:

- ½ cup bread crumbs
- ¼ tsp paprika
- Salt and pepper to taste
- ⅛ tsp dried sage
- ⅛ tsp garlic powder
- ¼ tsp ground cumin
- 1 egg
- 4 turkey breast cutlets
- 2 tbsp chopped chervil

Directions:

1. Preheat air fryer to 190°C/380°F.
2. Combine the bread crumbs, paprika, salt, black pepper, sage, cumin, and garlic powder in a bowl and mix well.
3. Beat the egg in another bowl until frothy.
4. Dip the turkey cutlets into the egg mixture, then coat them in the bread crumb mixture.
5. Put the breaded turkey cutlets in the air fryer basket. Bake for 4 minutes. Turn the cutlets over, then Bake for 4 more minutes.
6. Decorate with chervil and serve.

Variations & Ingredients Tips:

- Use chicken or pork cutlets instead of turkey for different proteins.
- Add grated Parmesan cheese or finely chopped nuts to the breading for extra flavor and crunch.
- Serve with a side of cranberry sauce, gravy, or roasted vegetables.

Per Serving: Calories: 200; Total Fat: 5g; Saturated Fat: 1g; Sodium: 220mg; Total Carbohydrates: 12g; Dietary Fiber: 1g; Total Sugars: 1g; Protein: 25g

Maewoon Chicken Legs

Servings: 4 | Prep Time: 10 Minutes | Cooking Time: 30 Minutes + Chilling Time

Ingredients:

- 4 scallions, sliced, whites and greens separated
- 1/4 cup tamari
- 2 tbsp sesame oil
- 1 tsp sesame seeds
- 1/4 cup honey
- 2 tbsp gochujang
- 2 tbsp ketchup
- 4 cloves garlic, minced
- 1/2 tsp ground ginger
- Salt and pepper to taste
- 1 tbsp parsley
- 680g chicken legs

Directions:

1. Whisk all ingredients, except chicken and scallion greens, in a bowl. Reserve 1/4 cup of marinade.
2. Toss chicken legs in the remaining marinade and chill for 30 minutes.
3. Preheat air fryer at 200°C/400°F. Place chicken legs in the greased frying basket and Air Fry for 10 minutes. Turn chicken. Cook for 8 more minutes.
4. Let sit in a serving dish for 5 minutes. Coat the cooked chicken with the reserved marinade and scatter with scallion greens, sesame seeds and parsley to serve.

Variations & Ingredients Tips:

- Use chicken wings or drumsticks instead of legs.
- Add a splash of rice vinegar or mirin to the marinade.
- Serve with steamed rice and kimchi.

Per Serving: Calories: 510; Total Fat: 32g; Saturated Fat: 8g; Cholesterol: 215mg; Sodium: 1510mg; Total Carbs: 23g; Dietary Fiber: 1g; Total Sugars: 19g; Protein: 35g

Cheesy Chicken-avocado Paninis

Servings: 2 | Prep Time: 15 Minutes | Cooking Time: 25 Minutes

Ingredients:

- 2 tbsp mayonnaise
- 4 tsp yellow mustard
- 4 sandwich bread slices
- 113 grams sliced deli chicken ham
- 57 grams sliced provolone cheese
- 57 grams sliced mozzarella
- 1 avocado, sliced
- 1 tomato, sliced
- Salt and pepper to taste
- 1 tsp sesame seeds
- 2 tbsp butter, melted

Directions:

1. Preheat air fryer at 180°C/350°F.
2. Rub mayonnaise and mustard on the inside of each bread slice.
3. Top 2 bread slices with chicken ham, provolone and mozzarella cheese, avocado, sesame seeds, and tomato slices. Season with salt and pepper. Then, close sandwiches with the remaining bread slices.
4. Brush the top and bottom of each sandwich lightly with melted butter.
5. Place sandwiches in the air fryer basket and Bake for 6 minutes, flipping once.
6. Serve.

Variations & Ingredients Tips:

- Substitute chicken ham with sliced turkey, roast beef, or bacon.
- Use pesto, hummus, or guacamole instead of mayonnaise and mustard.
- Add sliced onions, bell peppers, or pickles for extra crunch and flavor.

Per Serving: Calories: 680; Total Fat: 49g; Saturated Fat: 20g; Sodium: 1460mg; Total Carbohydrates: 32g; Dietary Fiber: 6g; Total Sugars: 6g; Protein: 32g

Parmesan Chicken Meatloaf

Servings: 4 | Prep Time: 15 Minutes | Cooking Time: 45 Minutes

Ingredients:

- 1 1/2 tsp evaporated cane sugar
- 450g ground chicken
- 4 garlic cloves, minced
- 2 tbsp grated Parmesan
- 1/4 cup heavy cream
- 1/4 cup minced onion
- 2 tbsp chopped basil

- 2 tbsp chopped parsley
- Salt and pepper to taste
- 1/2 tsp onion powder
- 1/2 cup bread crumbs
- 1/4 tsp red pepper flakes
- 1 egg
- 1 cup tomato sauce
- 1/2 tsp garlic powder
- 1/2 tsp dried thyme
- 1/2 tsp dried oregano
- 1 tbsp coconut aminos

Directions:

1. Preheat air fryer to 200°C/400°F.
2. Combine chicken, garlic, minced onion, oregano, thyme, basil, salt, pepper, onion powder, Parmesan cheese, red pepper flakes, bread crumbs, egg, and cream in a large bowl. Transfer the chicken mixture to a prepared baking dish.
3. Stir together tomato sauce, garlic powder, coconut aminos, and sugar in a small bowl. Spread over the meatloaf. Loosely cover with foil. Place the pan in the frying basket and bake for 15 minutes.
4. Take the foil off and bake for another 15 minutes.
5. Allow resting for 10 minutes before slicing. Serve sprinkled with parsley.

Variations & Ingredients Tips:

- Use ground turkey or pork instead of chicken.
- Add grated zucchini or carrots for extra veggies and moisture.
- Wrap bacon strips around the meatloaf before cooking.

Per Serving: Calories: 360; Total Fat: 21g; Saturated Fat: 8g; Cholesterol: 165mg; Sodium: 730mg; Total Carbs: 14g; Dietary Fiber: 1g; Total Sugars: 5g; Protein: 30g

Chicken Cutlets With Broccoli Rabe And Roasted Peppers

Servings: 2 | Prep Time: 10 Minutes | Cooking Time: 10 Minutes

Ingredients:

- 1/2 bunch broccoli rabe
- Olive oil, in a spray bottle
- Salt and freshly ground black pepper
- ⅔ cup roasted red pepper strips
- 2 (115g) boneless, skinless chicken breasts
- 2 tablespoons all-purpose flour
- 1 egg, beaten
- 1/3 cup seasoned breadcrumbs
- 2 slices aged provolone cheese

Directions:

1. Bring a medium saucepot of salted water to a boil on the stovetop. Blanch the broccoli rabe for 3 minutes in the boiling water and then drain. When it has cooled a little, squeeze out as much water as possible, drizzle a little olive oil on top, season with salt and black pepper and set aside. Dry the roasted red peppers with a clean kitchen towel and set them aside as well.
2. Place each chicken breast between 2 pieces of plastic wrap. Use a meat pounder to flatten the chicken breasts to about 1.3cm thick. Season the chicken on both sides with salt and pepper.
3. Preheat the air fryer to 205°C/400°F.
4. Set up a dredging station with three shallow dishes. Place the flour in one dish, the egg in a second dish and the breadcrumbs in a third dish. Coat the chicken on all sides with the flour. Shake off any excess flour and dip the chicken into the egg. Let the excess egg drip off and coat both sides of the chicken in the breadcrumbs. Spray the chicken with olive oil on both sides and transfer to the air fryer basket.
5. Air-fry the chicken at 205°C/400°F for 5 minutes. Turn the chicken over and air-fry for another minute. Then, top the chicken breast with the broccoli rabe and roasted peppers. Place a slice of the provolone cheese on top and secure it with a toothpick or two.
6. Air-fry at 180°C/360°F for 3 to 4 minutes to melt the cheese and warm everything together.

Variations & Ingredients Tips:

- Use spinach or kale instead of broccoli rabe.
- Substitute mozzarella or fontina cheese for the provolone.
- Add sliced mushrooms or onions to the vegetable topping.

Per Serving: Calories: 424; Total Fat: 16g; Saturated Fat: 6g; Cholesterol: 173mg; Sodium: 730mg; Total Carbs: 29g; Dietary Fiber: 3g; Total Sugars: 2g; Protein: 41g

Tandoori Chicken Legs

Servings: 2 | Prep Time: 10 Minutes + Marinating | Cooking Time: 30 Minutes

Ingredients:

- 1 cup plain yogurt
- 2 cloves garlic, minced
- 1 tablespoon grated fresh ginger
- 2 teaspoons paprika
- 2 teaspoons ground coriander
- 1 teaspoon ground turmeric
- 1 teaspoon salt
- 1/4 teaspoon ground cayenne pepper
- Juice of 1 lime
- 2 bone-in, skin-on chicken legs
- Fresh cilantro leaves

Directions:

1. Make marinade by combining yogurt, garlic, ginger, spices and lime juice.
2. Slash chicken legs and pour marinade over them. Refrigerate for at least 1 hour.
3. Preheat air fryer to 195°C/380°F.
4. Transfer chicken from marinade to air fryer basket, reserving extra marinade.
5. Air fry for 15 mins. Flip chicken and pour over remaining marinade.

6. Air fry 15 more mins, tenting with foil if browning too much.
7. Serve over rice with fresh cilantro.

Variations & Ingredients Tips:

- Use chicken thighs or breasts instead of legs.
- Add a dollop of yogurt or cream to finished dish for richness.
- Adjust cayenne amount to preference for heat level.

Per Serving (1 leg): Calories: 307; Total Fat: 13g; Saturated Fat: 4g; Cholesterol: 122mg; Sodium: 791mg; Total Carbs: 12g; Dietary Fiber: 1g; Total Sugars: 3g; Protein: 34g

Favorite Fried Chicken Wings

Servings: 4 | Prep Time: 15 Minutes | Cooking Time: 30 Minutes

Ingredients:

- 16 chicken wings
- 1 tsp garlic powder
- 1/2 tsp paprika
- 1 tsp chicken seasoning
- Black pepper to taste
- 1/2 cup flour
- 1/4 cup sour cream
- 2 tsp red chili flakes

Directions:

1. Preheat air fryer to 200°C/400°F.
2. Put the drumettes in a resealable bag along with garlic powder, chicken seasoning, paprika, and pepper. Seal the bag and shake until the chicken is completely coated.
3. Prepare a clean resealable bag and add the flour. Pour sour cream in a large bowl.
4. Dunk the drumettes into the sour cream, then transfer them to the bag of flour. Seal the bag and shake until coated and repeat until all of the wings are coated.
5. Transfer the drumettes to the frying basket. Lightly spray them with cooking oil and Air Fry for 23-25 minutes, shaking the basket a few times until crispy and golden brown.
6. Allow to cool slightly. Sprinkle with red chili flakes and serve.

Variations & Ingredients Tips:

- Toss the cooked wings in your favorite wing sauce like Buffalo or BBQ.
- Marinate the wings overnight in buttermilk for extra tenderness.
- Serve with celery sticks and blue cheese dressing.

Per Serving: Calories: 470; Total Fat: 32g; Saturated Fat: 10g; Cholesterol: 155mg; Sodium: 620mg; Total Carbs: 14g; Dietary Fiber: 1g; Total Sugars: 1g; Protein: 33g

Turkey Scotch Eggs

Servings: 4 | Prep Time: 20 Minutes | Cooking Time: 30 Minutes

Ingredients:

- 680g ground turkey
- 1 tbsp ground cumin
- 1 tsp ground coriander
- 2 garlic cloves, minced
- 3 raw eggs
- 1 1/2 cups bread crumbs
- 6 hard-cooked eggs, peeled
- 1/2 cup flour

Directions:

1. Preheat air fryer to 190°C/370°F.
2. Place the ground turkey, cumin, coriander, garlic, one egg, and 1/2 cup of bread crumbs in a large bowl and mix until well incorporated.
3. Divide into 6 equal portions, then flatten each into long ovals. Set aside.
4. In a shallow bowl, beat the remaining raw eggs. In another shallow bowl, add flour. Do the same with another plate for bread crumbs.
5. Roll each cooked egg in flour, then wrap with one oval of chicken sausage until completely covered.
6. Roll again in flour, then coat in the beaten egg before rolling in bread crumbs.
7. Arrange the eggs in the greased frying basket. Air Fry for 12-14 minutes, flipping once until the sausage is cooked and the eggs are brown.
8. Serve.

Variations & Ingredients Tips:

- Use ground pork or beef instead of turkey.
- Add some cayenne pepper or smoked paprika to the meat mixture.
- Serve with a spicy mustard or Sriracha mayo dipping sauce.

Per Serving: Calories: 500; Total Fat: 26g; Saturated Fat: 7g; Cholesterol: 435mg; Sodium: 620mg; Total Carbs: 30g; Dietary Fiber: 2g; Total Sugars: 3g; Protein: 37g

Indian Chicken Tandoori

Servings: 2 | Prep Time: 10 Minutes (plus Marinating Time) | Cooking Time: 35 Minutes

Ingredients:

- 2 chicken breasts, cubed
- 1/2 cup hung curd
- 1 tsp turmeric powder
- 1 tsp red chili powder
- 1 tsp chaat masala powder
- Pinch of salt

Directions:

1. Preheat air fryer to 175°C/350°F.
2. Mix the hung curd, turmeric, red chili powder, chaat masala powder, and salt in a mixing bowl. Stir until the mixture is free of lumps.

3. Coat the chicken with the mixture, cover, and refrigerate for 30 minutes to marinate.
4. Place the marinated chicken chunks in a baking pan and drizzle with the remaining marinade.
5. Bake for 25 minutes until the chicken is juicy and spiced.
6. Serve warm.

Variations & Ingredients Tips:

- Use Greek yogurt instead of hung curd for a tangy flavor.
- Add minced garlic and ginger to the marinade for extra zing.
- Garnish with fresh cilantro and squeeze of lime juice.

Per Serving: Calories: 220; Total Fat: 3g; Saturated Fat: 1g; Cholesterol: 105mg; Sodium: 370mg; Total Carbs: 4g; Dietary Fiber: 1g; Total Sugars: 2g; Protein: 41g

Chicken Schnitzel Dogs

Servings: 4 | Prep Time: 20 Minutes | Cooking Time: 10 Minutes

Ingredients:

- ½ cup flour
- ½ teaspoon salt
- 1 teaspoon marjoram
- 1 teaspoon dried parsley flakes
- ½ teaspoon thyme
- 1 egg
- 1 teaspoon lemon juice
- 1 teaspoon water
- 1 cup breadcrumbs
- 4 chicken tenders, pounded thin
- oil for misting or cooking spray
- 4 whole-grain hotdog buns
- 4 slices Gouda cheese
- 1 small Granny Smith apple, thinly sliced
- ½ cup shredded Napa cabbage
- coleslaw dressing

Directions:

1. In a shallow dish, mix together the flour, salt, marjoram, parsley, and thyme.
2. In another shallow dish, beat together egg, lemon juice, and water.
3. Place breadcrumbs in a third shallow dish.
4. Cut each of the flattened chicken tenders in half lengthwise.
5. Dip flattened chicken strips in flour mixture, then egg wash. Let excess egg drip off and roll in breadcrumbs. Spray both sides with oil or cooking spray.
6. Cook at 200°C/390°F for 5 minutes. Spray with oil, turn over, and spray other side.
7. Cook for 3 to 5 minutes more, until well done and crispy brown.
8. To serve, place 2 schnitzel strips on bottom of each hot dog bun. Top with cheese, sliced apple, and cabbage. Drizzle with coleslaw dressing and top with other half of bun.

Variations & Ingredients Tips:

- Use turkey or pork cutlets instead of chicken for different schnitzel options.
- Add sauerkraut, pickles, or mustard for German-style toppings.
- Serve with a side of potato salad or French fries.

Per Serving: Calories: 480; Total Fat: 20g; Saturated Fat: 6g; Sodium: 1020mg; Total Carbohydrates: 48g; Dietary Fiber: 6g; Total Sugars: 9g; Protein: 31g

Sticky Drumsticks

Servings: 4 | Prep Time: 10 Minutes | Cooking Time: 45 Minutes

Ingredients:

- 450-g chicken drumsticks
- 1 tbsp chicken seasoning
- 1 tsp dried chili flakes
- Salt and pepper to taste
- 1/4 cup honey
- 1 cup barbecue sauce

Directions:

1. Preheat air fryer to 200°C/390°F.
2. Season drumsticks with chicken seasoning, chili flakes, salt, and pepper.
3. Place one batch of drumsticks in the greased frying basket and Air Fry for 18-20 minutes, flipping once until golden.
4. While the chicken is cooking, combine honey and barbecue sauce in a small bowl.
5. Remove the drumsticks to a serving dish. Drizzle honey-barbecue sauce over and serve.

Variations & Ingredients Tips:

- Use chicken wings or thighs instead of drumsticks.
- Add garlic powder or smoked paprika to the seasoning blend.
- Brush sauce on the chicken halfway through cooking for extra stickiness.

Per Serving (3 drumsticks): Calories: 374; Total Fat: 9g; Saturated Fat: 2g; Cholesterol: 132mg; Sodium: 833mg; Total Carbs: 49g; Dietary Fiber: 1g; Total Sugars: 41g; Protein: 27g

Crispy Duck With Cherry Sauce

Servings: 2 | Prep Time: 20 Minutes | Cooking Time: 33 Minutes

Ingredients:

- 1 whole duck (up to 2.3 kg), split in half, back and rib bones removed
- 1 teaspoon olive oil
- salt and freshly ground black pepper
- Cherry Sauce:
- 1 tablespoon butter
- 1 shallot, minced
- ½ cup sherry
- ¾ cup cherry preserves
- 1 cup chicken stock
- 1 teaspoon white wine vinegar

- 1 teaspoon fresh thyme leaves
- salt and freshly ground black pepper

Directions:

1. Preheat the air fryer to 200°C/400°F.
2. Trim some of the fat from the duck. Rub olive oil on the duck and season with salt and pepper. Place the duck halves in the air fryer basket, breast side up and facing the center of the basket.
3. Air-fry the duck for 20 minutes. Turn the duck over and air-fry for another 6 minutes.
4. While duck is air-frying, make the cherry sauce. Melt the butter in a large sauté pan. Add the shallot and sauté until it is just starting to brown – about 2 to 3 minutes. Add the sherry and deglaze the pan by scraping up any brown bits from the bottom of the pan. Simmer the liquid for a few minutes, until it has reduced by half. Add the cherry preserves, chicken stock and white wine vinegar. Whisk well to combine all the ingredients. Simmer the sauce until it thickens and coats the back of a spoon – about 5 to 7 minutes. Season with salt and pepper and stir in the fresh thyme leaves.
5. When the air fryer timer goes off, spoon some cherry sauce over the duck and continue to air-fry at 200°C/400°F for 4 more minutes. Then, turn the duck halves back over so that the breast side is facing up. Spoon more cherry sauce over the top of the duck, covering the skin completely. Air-fry for 3 more minutes and then remove the duck to a plate to rest for a few minutes.
6. Serve the duck in halves, or cut each piece in half again for a smaller serving. Spoon any additional sauce over the duck or serve it on the side.

Variations & Ingredients Tips:

- Use duck breasts or legs instead of a whole duck for quicker cooking time.
- Substitute cherry preserves with blackberry, raspberry, or apricot jam.
- Garnish with fresh herbs like rosemary, sage, or parsley before serving.

Per Serving: Calories: 610; Total Fat: 36g; Saturated Fat: 12g; Sodium: 430mg; Total Carbohydrates: 41g; Dietary Fiber: 1g; Total Sugars: 34g; Protein: 34g

Restaurant-style Chicken Thighs

Servings: 4 | Prep Time: 5 Minutes (plus 10 Minutes Marinating Time) | Cooking Time: 30 Minutes

Ingredients:

- 454 grams boneless, skinless chicken thighs
- ¼ cup barbecue sauce
- 2 cloves garlic, minced
- 1 tsp lemon zest
- 2 tbsp parsley, chopped
- 2 tbsp lemon juice

Directions:

1. Coat the chicken with barbecue sauce, garlic, and lemon juice in a medium bowl. leave to marinate for 10 minutes.
2. Preheat air fryer to 190°C/380°F.
3. When ready to cook, remove the chicken from the bowl and shake off any drips. Arrange the chicken in the air fryer and Bake for 16-18 minutes, until golden and cooked through.
4. Serve topped with lemon zest and parsley. Enjoy!

Variations & Ingredients Tips:

- Use honey mustard, teriyaki, or pesto sauce instead of BBQ for different flavors.
- Add sliced onions, peppers, or mushrooms to the marinade for extra veggies.
- Serve with sweet potato fries, coleslaw, or grilled corn on the side.

Per Serving: Calories: 250; Total Fat: 11g; Saturated Fat: 2.5g; Sodium: 440mg; Total Carbohydrates: 8g; Dietary Fiber: 0g; Total Sugars: 6g; Protein: 29g

Saucy Chicken Thighs

Servings: 4 | Prep Time: 10 Minutes | Cooking Time: 35 Minutes

Ingredients:

- 8 boneless, skinless chicken thighs
- 1 tbsp Italian seasoning
- Salt and pepper to taste
- 2 garlic cloves, minced
- ½ tsp apple cider vinegar
- ½ cup honey
- ¼ cup Dijon mustard

Directions:

1. Preheat air fryer to 200°C/400°F.
2. Season the chicken with Italian seasoning, salt, and black pepper. Place in the greased air fryer basket and Bake for 15 minutes, flipping once halfway through cooking.
3. While the chicken is cooking, add garlic, honey, vinegar, and Dijon mustard in a saucepan and stir-fry over medium heat for 4 minutes or until the sauce has thickened and warmed through.
4. Transfer the thighs to a serving dish and drizzle with honey-mustard sauce.
5. Serve and enjoy!

Variations & Ingredients Tips:

- Use bone-in, skin-on chicken thighs for crispier skin and juicier meat.
- Substitute Dijon mustard with grainy mustard or spicy brown mustard for a different flavor.
- Serve with roasted potatoes, green beans, or a side salad.

Per Serving: Calories: 400; Total Fat: 14g; Saturated Fat:

3.5g; Sodium: 550mg; Total Carbohydrates: 34g; Dietary Fiber: 0g; Total Sugars: 32g; Protein: 37g

Popcorn Chicken Tenders With Vegetables

Servings: 4 | Prep Time: 15 Minutes | Cooking Time: 30 Minutes

Ingredients:

- 2 tbsp cooked popcorn, ground
- Salt and pepper to taste
- 450g chicken tenders
- 1/2 cup bread crumbs
- 1/2 tsp dried thyme
- 1 tbsp olive oil
- 2 carrots, sliced
- 12 baby potatoes

Directions:

1. Preheat air fryer to 190°C/380°F.
2. Season the chicken tenders with salt and pepper.
3. In a shallow bowl, mix the crumbs, popcorn, thyme, and olive oil until combined. Coat the chicken with mixture. Press firmly, so the crumbs adhere.
4. Arrange the carrots and baby potatoes in the greased frying basket and top them with the chicken tenders.
5. Bake for 9-10 minutes. Shake the basket and continue cooking for another 9-10 minutes, until the vegetables are tender.
6. Serve and enjoy!

Variations & Ingredients Tips:

- Use crushed corn flakes or potato chips instead of popcorn.
- Add some garlic powder, paprika or parmesan to the breading.
- Serve with honey mustard, BBQ sauce or ranch for dipping.

Per Serving: Calories: 320; Total Fat: 9g; Saturated Fat: 1.5g; Cholesterol: 85mg; Sodium: 280mg; Total Carbs: 30g; Dietary Fiber: 3g; Total Sugars: 2g; Protein: 31g

Coconut Curry Chicken With Coconut Rice

Servings: 4 | Prep Time: 20 Minutes (plus Marinating Time) | Cooking Time: 56 Minutes

Ingredients:

- 1 (400-ml) can coconut milk
- 2 tablespoons green or red curry paste
- Zest and juice of one lime
- 1 clove garlic, minced
- 1 tablespoon grated fresh ginger
- 1 teaspoon ground cumin
- 1 (1.4 to 1.8-kg) chicken, cut into 8 pieces
- Vegetable or olive oil
- Salt and freshly ground black pepper
- Fresh cilantro leaves
- For the rice:
- 1 cup basmati or jasmine rice
- 1 cup water
- 1 cup coconut milk
- 1/2 teaspoon salt
- Freshly ground black pepper

Directions:

1. Make the marinade by combining the coconut milk, curry paste, lime zest and juice, garlic, ginger and cumin. Coat the chicken on all sides with the marinade and marinate the chicken for 1 hour to overnight in the refrigerator.
2. Preheat the air fryer to 190°C/380°F.
3. Brush the bottom of the air fryer basket with oil. Transfer the chicken thighs and drumsticks from the marinade to the air fryer basket, letting most of the marinade drip off. Season to taste with salt and freshly ground black pepper.
4. Air-fry the chicken drumsticks and thighs at 190°C/380°F for 12 minutes. Flip the chicken over and continue to air-fry for another 12 minutes. Set aside and air-fry the chicken breast pieces at 190°C/380°F for 15 minutes. Turn the chicken breast pieces over and air-fry for another 12 minutes. Return the chicken thighs and drumsticks to the air fryer and air-fry for an additional 5 minutes.
5. While the chicken is cooking, make the coconut rice. Rinse the rice kernels with water and drain well. Place the rice in a medium saucepan with a tight fitting lid, along with the water, coconut milk, salt and freshly ground black pepper. Bring the mixture to a boil and then cover, reduce the heat and let it cook gently for 20 minutes without lifting the lid. When the time is up, lift the lid, fluff with a fork and set aside.
6. Remove the chicken from the air fryer and serve warm with the coconut rice and fresh cilantro scattered around.

Variations & Ingredients Tips:

- Adjust the amount of curry paste to your spice preference.
- Use boneless, skinless chicken thighs for a quicker cooking time.
- Garnish with chopped peanuts or cashews for extra crunch.

Per Serving: Calories: 670; Total Fat: 42g; Saturated Fat: 29g; Cholesterol: 150mg; Sodium: 580mg; Total Carbs: 34g; Dietary Fiber: 1g; Total Sugars: 1g; Protein: 40g

Herb-marinated Chicken

Servings: 4 | Prep Time: 10 Minutes (plus Marinating Time) | Cooking Time: 25 Minutes

Ingredients:

- 4 chicken breasts
- 2 tsp rosemary, minced
- 2 tsp thyme, minced
- Salt and pepper to taste
- 1/2 cup chopped cilantro
- 1 lime, juiced

Directions:

1. Place chicken in a resealable bag. Add rosemary, thyme, salt, pepper, cilantro, and lime juice. Seal the bag and toss to coat, then place in the refrigerator for 2 hours.
2. Preheat air fryer to 200°C/400°F.
3. Arrange the chicken in a single layer in the greased frying basket. Spray the chicken with cooking oil.
4. Air Fry for 6-7 minutes, then flip the chicken. Cook for another 3 minutes.
5. Serve and enjoy!

Variations & Ingredients Tips:

- Substitute cilantro with parsley or basil.
- Add a tablespoon of honey or mustard to the marinade.
- Slice the cooked chicken and serve over salad or in wraps.

Per Serving: Calories: 170; Total Fat: 3g; Saturated Fat: 0.5g; Cholesterol: 85mg; Sodium: 75mg; Total Carbs: 1g; Dietary Fiber: 0g; Total Sugars: 0g; Protein: 32g

Spinach And Feta Stuffed Chicken Breasts

Servings: 4 | Prep Time: 15 Minutes | Cooking Time: 27 Minutes

Ingredients:

- 1 (285g) package frozen spinach, thawed and drained well
- 1 cup feta cheese, crumbled
- 1/2 teaspoon freshly ground black pepper
- 4 boneless chicken breasts
- Salt and freshly ground black pepper
- 1 tablespoon olive oil

Directions:

1. Prepare the filling. Squeeze out as much liquid as possible from the thawed spinach. Rough chop the spinach and transfer it to a mixing bowl with the feta cheese and the freshly ground black pepper.
2. Prepare the chicken breast. Place the chicken breast on a cutting board and press down on the chicken breast with one hand to keep it stabilized. Make an incision about 2.5cm long in the fattest side of the breast. Move the knife up and down inside the chicken breast, without poking through either the top or the bottom, or the other side of the breast. The inside pocket should be about 7.5cm long, but the opening should only be about 2.5cm wide. If this is too difficult, you can make the incision longer, but you will have to be more careful when cooking the chicken breast since this will expose more of the stuffing.
3. Once you have prepared the chicken breasts, use your fingers to stuff the filling into each pocket, spreading the mixture down as far as you can.
4. Preheat the air fryer to 195°C/380°F.
5. Lightly brush or spray the air fryer basket and the chicken breasts with olive oil. Transfer two of the stuffed chicken breasts to the air fryer. Air-fry for 12 minutes, turning the chicken breasts over halfway through the cooking time. Remove the chicken to a resting plate and air-fry the second two breasts for 12 minutes. Return the first batch of chicken to the air fryer with the second batch and air-fry for 3 more minutes. When the chicken is cooked, an instant read thermometer should register 75°C/165°F in the thickest part of the chicken, as well as in the stuffing.
6. Remove the chicken breasts and let them rest on a cutting board for 2 to 3 minutes. Slice the chicken on the bias and serve with the slices fanned out.

Variations & Ingredients Tips:

- Use fresh spinach instead of frozen.
- Substitute feta for goat cheese or shredded mozzarella.
- Add sun-dried tomatoes or pine nuts to the stuffing mixture.

Per Serving: Calories: 332; Total Fat: 14g; Saturated Fat: 7g; Cholesterol: 143mg; Sodium: 599mg; Total Carbs: 6g; Dietary Fiber: 2g; Total Sugars: 2g; Protein: 44g

Cheesy Chicken Tenders

Servings: 4 | Prep Time: 15 Minutes | Cooking Time: 25 Minutes

Ingredients:

- 1 cup grated Parmesan cheese
- ¼ cup grated cheddar
- 567 grams chicken tenders
- 1 egg, beaten
- 2 tbsp milk
- Salt and pepper to taste
- ½ tsp garlic powder
- 1 tsp dried thyme
- ¼ tsp shallot powder

Directions:

1. Preheat the air fryer to 200°C/400°F.
2. Stir the egg and milk until combined. Mix the salt, pepper, garlic, thyme, shallot, cheddar cheese, and Parmesan cheese on a plate.
3. Dip the chicken in the egg mix, then in the cheese mix, and press to coat.
4. Lay the tenders in the air fryer basket in a single layer. Add a raised rack to cook more at one time. Spray all with oil and Bake for 12-16 minutes, flipping once halfway through cooking.
5. Serve hot.

Variations & Ingredients Tips:

- Use panko breadcrumbs or crushed cornflakes instead of cheese for a different crust.
- Add a pinch of cayenne pepper or paprika to the coating for a spicy kick.
- Serve with honey mustard, ranch, or marinara sauce for

dipping.

Per Serving: Calories: 420; Total Fat: 21g; Saturated Fat: 9g; Sodium: 860mg; Total Carbohydrates: 4g; Dietary Fiber: 0g; Total Sugars: 1g; Protein: 51g

Super-simple Herby Turkey

Servings: 4 | Prep Time: 10 Minutes | Cooking Time: 35 Minutes

Ingredients:

- 2 turkey tenderloins
- 2 tbsp olive oil
- Salt and pepper to taste
- 2 tbsp minced rosemary
- 1 tbsp minced thyme
- 1 tbsp minced sage

Directions:

1. Preheat the air fryer to 175°C/350°F.
2. Brush the tenderloins with olive oil and sprinkle with salt and pepper.
3. Mix rosemary, thyme, and sage, then rub the seasoning onto the meat.
4. Put the tenderloins in the frying basket and Bake for 22-27 minutes, flipping once until cooked through.
5. Lay the turkey on a serving plate, cover with foil, and let stand for 5 minutes. Slice before serving.

Variations & Ingredients Tips:

- Use a turkey breast instead of tenderloins, adjusting cooking time.
- Add garlic powder or onion powder to the herb mix.
- Brush with melted butter before cooking for extra richness.

Per Serving: Calories: 196; Total Fat: 7g; Saturated Fat: 1g; Cholesterol: 91mg; Sodium: 90mg; Total Carbs: 1g; Dietary Fiber: 0g; Total Sugars: 0g; Protein: 31g

Guajillo Chile Chicken Meatballs

Servings: 4 | Prep Time: 10 Minutes | Cooking Time: 30 Minutes

Ingredients:

- 450g ground chicken
- 1 large egg
- 1/2 cup bread crumbs
- 1 tbsp sour cream
- 2 tsp brown mustard
- 2 tbsp grated onion
- 2 tbsp tomato paste
- 1 tsp ground cumin
- 1 tsp guajillo chile powder
- 2 tbsp olive oil

Directions:

1. Preheat air fryer to 175°C/350°F.
2. Mix the ground chicken, egg, bread crumbs, sour cream, mustard, onion, tomato paste, cumin, and chili powder in a bowl. Form into 16 meatballs.
3. Place the meatballs in the greased frying basket and Air Fry for 8-10 minutes, shaking once until browned and cooked through.
4. Serve immediately.

Variations & Ingredients Tips:

- Use ground turkey for a leaner option.
- Add some minced garlic or cilantro to the mix.
- Serve with salsa, guacamole or queso fresco.

Per Serving: Calories: 330; Total Fat: 22g; Saturated Fat: 5g; Cholesterol: 165mg; Sodium: 270mg; Total Carbs: 7g; Dietary Fiber: 1g; Total Sugars: 2g; Protein: 27g

Enchilada Chicken Quesadillas

Servings: 4 | Prep Time: 15 Minutes | Cooking Time: 35 Minutes

Ingredients:

- 2 cups cooked chicken breasts, shredded
- 1 can (120g) diced green chilies, including juice
- 2 cups grated Mexican cheese blend
- 3/4 cup sour cream
- 2 tsp chili powder
- 1 tsp cumin
- 1 tbsp chipotle sauce
- 1 tsp dried onion flakes
- 1/2 tsp salt
- 3 tbsp butter, melted
- 8 flour tortillas

Directions:

1. In a small bowl, whisk the sour cream, chipotle sauce and chili powder. Let chill in the fridge until ready to use.
2. Preheat air fryer at 175°C/350°F.
3. Mix the chicken, green chilies, cumin, and salt in a bowl. Set aside.
4. Brush on one side of a tortilla lightly with melted butter. Layer with 1/4 cup of chicken, onion flakes and 1/4 cup of Mexican cheese. Top with a second tortilla and lightly brush with butter on top. Repeat with the remaining ingredients.
5. Place quesadillas, butter side down, in the frying basket and Bake for 3 minutes.
6. Cut them into 6 sections and serve with cream sauce on the side.

Variations & Ingredients Tips:

- Use corn tortillas for a gluten-free option.
- Add sautéed bell peppers and onions to the chicken mixture.
- Top with sliced avocado, salsa and cilantro.

Per Serving: Calories: 660; Total Fat: 41g; Saturated Fat: 22g; Cholesterol: 160mg; Sodium: 1230mg; Total Carbs: 35g; Dietary Fiber: 2g; Total Sugars: 3g; Protein: 37g

Japanese-style Turkey Meatballs

Servings: 4 | Prep Time: 15 Minutes | Cooking Time: 25 Minutes

Ingredients:

- 600g ground turkey
- 1/4 cup panko bread crumbs
- 4 chopped scallions
- 1/4 cup chopped cilantro
- 1 egg
- 1 tbsp grated ginger
- 1 garlic clove, minced
- 3 tbsp shoyu
- 2 tsp toasted sesame oil
- 3/4 tsp salt
- 2 tbsp oyster sauce
- 2 tbsp fresh orange juice

Directions:

1. Add ground turkey, panko, 3 scallions, cilantro, egg, ginger, garlic, 1 tbsp of shoyu sauce, sesame oil, and salt in a bowl. Mix with hands until combined.
2. Divide the mixture into 12 equal parts and roll into balls.
3. Preheat air fryer to 190°C/380°F. Place the meatballs in the greased frying basket. Bake for about 9-11 minutes, flipping once until browned and cooked through. Repeat for all meatballs.
4. In a small saucepan over medium heat, add oyster sauce, orange juice and remaining shoyu sauce. Bring to a boil, then reduce the heat to low. Cook until the sauce is slightly reduced, 3 minutes.
5. Serve the meatballs with the oyster sauce drizzled over them and topped with the remaining scallions.

Variations & Ingredients Tips:

- Use ground chicken or pork instead of turkey.
- Add some Sriracha to the sauce for heat.
- Serve as an appetizer with toothpicks or in a bahn mi sandwich.

Per Serving: Calories: 330; Total Fat: 17g; Saturated Fat: 4g; Cholesterol: 130mg; Sodium: 1350mg; Total Carbs: 9g; Dietary Fiber: 1g; Total Sugars: 4g; Protein: 35g

Fish And Seafood Recipes

Holiday Shrimp Scampi

Servings: 4 | Prep Time: 10 Minutes | Cooking Time: 25 Minutes

Ingredients:

- 680g peeled shrimp, deveined
- 1/4 tsp lemon pepper seasoning
- 6 garlic cloves, minced
- 1 tsp salt
- 1/2 tsp grated lemon zest
- 3 tbsp fresh lemon juice
- 3 tbsp sunflower oil
- 3 tbsp butter
- 2 tsp fresh thyme leaves
- 1 lemon, cut into wedges

Directions:

1. Preheat air fryer to 200°C/400°F.
2. Combine shrimp, garlic, salt and lemon pepper in a pan. Toss to coat.
3. Add lemon zest, juice, oil and butter. Mix well.
4. Place pan in air fryer basket and bake for 10-13 mins, stirring once, until shrimp is opaque.
5. Sprinkle with thyme and serve with lemon wedges.

Variations & Ingredients Tips:

- Add red pepper flakes for a kick of heat.
- Toss shrimp with parmesan before serving.
- Serve over pasta, rice or with crusty bread.

Per Serving: Calories: 285; Total Fat: 16g; Saturated Fat: 5g; Cholesterol: 285mg; Sodium: 1180mg; Total Carbs: 6g; Dietary Fiber: 1g; Total Sugars: 1g; Protein: 29g

Sweet & Spicy Swordfish Kebabs

Servings: 4 | Prep Time: 15 Minutes | Cooking Time: 30 Minutes

Ingredients:

- ½ cup canned pineapple chunks, drained, juice reserved
- 453g swordfish steaks, cubed
- ½ cup large red grapes
- 1 tbsp honey
- 2 tsp grated fresh ginger
- 1 tsp olive oil
- Pinch cayenne pepper

Directions:

1. Preheat air fryer to 190°C/370°F.
2. Poke 8 bamboo skewers through the swordfish, pineapple, and grapes.
3. Mix the honey, 1 tbsp of pineapple juice, ginger, olive oil, and cayenne in a bowl, then use a brush to rub the mix on

the kebabs. Allow the marinade to sit on the kebabs for 10 minutes.

4. Grill the kebabs for 8-12 minutes until the fish is cooked through and the fruit is soft and glazed. Brush the kebabs again with the mix, then toss the rest of the marinade.
5. Serve warm and enjoy!

Variations & Ingredients Tips:

- Use mango or peach chunks instead of pineapple for a different tropical flavor.
- Add some red bell pepper pieces to the skewers for color and crunch.
- Sprinkle with chopped cilantro or mint before serving for freshness.

Per Serving: Calories: 220; Total Fat: 5g; Saturated Fat: 1g; Cholesterol: 65mg; Sodium: 180mg; Total Carbohydrates: 15g; Dietary Fiber: 1g; Total Sugars: 12g; Protein: 28g

Korean-style Fried Calamari

Servings: 4 | Prep Time: 15 Minutes | Cooking Time: 25 Minutes

Ingredients:

- 2 tbsp tomato paste
- 1 tbsp gochujang
- 1 tbsp lime juice
- 1 tsp lime zest
- 1 tsp smoked paprika
- 1/2 tsp salt
- 1 cup bread crumbs
- 150g calamari rings

Directions:

1. Preheat air fryer to 200°C/400°F.
2. Whisk tomato paste, gochujang, lime juice and zest, paprika, and salt in a bowl. In another bowl, add in the bread crumbs.
3. Dredge calamari rings in the tomato mixture, shake off excess, then roll through the crumbs.
4. Place calamari rings in the greased frying basket and Air Fry for 4-5 minutes, flipping once.
5. Serve.

Variations & Ingredients Tips:

- Add some grated garlic or ginger to the tomato mixture.
- Substitute gochujang with sriracha or sambal oelek.
- Serve with a sweet chili dipping sauce or soy-ginger aioli.

Per Serving: Calories: 180; Total Fat: 3g; Saturated Fat: 0.5g; Cholesterol: 265mg; Sodium: 860mg; Total Carbs: 25g; Dietary Fiber: 1g; Total Sugars: 3g; Protein: 14g

Quick Shrimp Scampi

Servings: 2 | Prep Time: 10 Minutes | Cooking Time: 5 Minutes

Ingredients:

- 16-20 large shrimp, peeled, deveined, tails removed
- 1/2 cup white wine
- Freshly ground black pepper
- 1/4 cup + 1 tablespoon butter, divided
- 1 clove garlic, sliced
- 1 teaspoon olive oil
- Salt, to taste
- Juice of 1/2 lemon, to taste
- 1/4 cup chopped fresh parsley

Directions:

1. Marinate shrimp in white wine and black pepper for 30 mins to 2 hrs, refrigerated.
2. Preheat air fryer to 200°C/400°F.
3. Melt 1/4 cup butter in a saucepan. Add garlic and simmer.
4. Pour shrimp and marinade into air fryer drawer. Drizzle shrimp with olive oil and season with salt.
5. Air-fry 3 mins. Turn shrimp over and pour garlic butter over top. Air-fry 2 more mins.
6. Transfer shrimp to a bowl. Toss with lemon juice, parsley and remaining 1 tbsp butter.

Variations & Ingredients Tips:

- Add red pepper flakes for some heat.
- Serve over pasta, rice or garlic bread.
- Use dry white wine for best flavor.

Per Serving: Calories: 325; Total Fat: 27g; Saturated Fat: 14g; Cholesterol: 250mg; Sodium: 590mg; Total Carbs: 3g; Dietary Fiber: 0g; Sugars: 0g; Protein: 15g

Better Fish Sticks

Servings: 3 | Prep Time: 10 Minutes | Cooking Time: 8 Minutes

Ingredients:

- ¾ cup Seasoned Italian-style dried bread crumbs (gluten-free, if a concern)
- 3 tablespoons (about 15g) finely grated Parmesan cheese
- 280g skinless cod fillets, cut lengthwise into 2.5-cm-wide pieces
- 3 tablespoons regular or low-fat mayonnaise (not fat-free; gluten-free, if a concern)
- Vegetable oil spray

Directions:

1. Preheat the air fryer to 200°C/400°F.
2. Mix the bread crumbs and grated Parmesan in a shallow soup bowl or a small pie plate.
3. Smear the fish fillet sticks completely with the mayonnaise, then dip them one by one in the bread-crumb mixture, turning and pressing gently to make an even and thorough coating. Coat each stick on all sides with vegetable oil spray.

4. Set the fish sticks in the basket with at least 6 mm between them. Air-fry undisturbed for 8 minutes, or until golden brown and crisp.
5. Use a nonstick-safe spatula to gently transfer them from the basket to a wire rack. Cool for only a minute or two before serving.

Variations & Ingredients Tips:

- Use salmon, tilapia or haddock instead of cod.
- Add some garlic powder, paprika or Old Bay seasoning to the breading mix.
- Serve with tartar sauce, ketchup or honey mustard for dipping.

Per Serving: Calories: 270; Total Fat: 12g; Saturated Fat: 2.5g; Cholesterol: 70mg; Sodium: 620mg; Total Carbs: 18g; Dietary Fiber: 1g; Total Sugars: 2g; Protein: 23g

Salmon

Servings: 4 | Prep Time: 5 Minutes | Cooking Time: 8 Minutes

Ingredients:

- Marinade
- 3 tablespoons low-sodium soy sauce
- 3 tablespoons rice vinegar
- 3 tablespoons ketchup
- 3 tablespoons olive oil
- 3 tablespoons brown sugar
- 1 teaspoon garlic powder
- 1/2 teaspoon ground ginger
- 4 (115-170g) salmon fillets (1.3cm thick)
- Cooking spray

Directions:

1. Mix all marinade ingredients until blended.
2. Place salmon in bag/container. Pour marinade over and coat well. Refrigerate 30 mins.
3. Drain marinade and spray air fryer basket with cooking spray.
4. Place salmon in basket, skin-side down.
5. Cook at 180°C/360°F for 10 mins, watching to avoid overcooking. Salmon is done when beginning to flake but still moist.

Variations & Ingredients Tips:

- Use teriyaki or pineapple marinade instead.
- Add sesame seeds or chopped green onions on top.
- Brush with additional marinade halfway through cooking.

Per Serving: Calories: 330; Total Fat: 18g; Saturated Fat: 3g; Cholesterol: 85mg; Sodium: 430mg; Total Carbs: 12g; Dietary Fiber: 0g; Sugars: 10g; Protein: 29g

Coconut-shrimp Po' Boys

Servings: 4 | Prep Time: 15 Minutes | Cooking Time: 5 Minutes

Ingredients:

- 1/2 cup cornstarch
- 2 eggs
- 2 tablespoons milk
- 3/4 cup shredded coconut
- 1/2 cup panko breadcrumbs
- 450g (31-35 count) shrimp, peeled and deveined
- Old Bay Seasoning
- Oil for misting or cooking spray
- 2 large hoagie rolls
- Honey mustard or light mayonnaise
- 1 1/2 cups shredded lettuce
- 1 large tomato, thinly sliced

Directions:

1. Place cornstarch in a shallow dish.
2. In another dish, beat eggs and milk.
3. In a third dish mix coconut and panko crumbs.
4. Season shrimp with Old Bay.
5. Dip shrimp in cornstarch, egg, then coconut mixture.
6. Mist shrimp with oil on both sides.
7. Air fry half the shrimp for 5 mins at 200°C/390°F.
8. Repeat for remaining shrimp.
9. To Assemble:
10. 1. Split hoagies, leaving one edge intact.
11. 2. Air fry 1-2 mins until heated.
12. 3. Spread with honey mustard/mayo.
13. 4. Top with lettuce, tomato and shrimp.

Variations & Ingredients Tips:

- Use cajun seasoning or garlic powder instead of Old Bay.
- Add sliced pickles or remoulade sauce.
- Serve on regular sandwich rolls instead of hoagies.

Per Serving: Calories: 389; Total Fat: 10g; Saturated Fat: 3g; Cholesterol: 225mg; Sodium: 662mg; Total Carbs: 45g; Dietary Fiber: 3g; Total Sugars: 5g; Protein: 29g

Horseradish Crusted Salmon

Servings: 2 | Prep Time: 10 Minutes | Cooking Time: 14 Minutes

Ingredients:

- 2 (140g) salmon fillets
- Salt and freshly ground black pepper
- 2 teaspoons Dijon mustard
- 1/2 cup panko breadcrumbs
- 2 tablespoons prepared horseradish
- 1/2 teaspoon finely chopped lemon zest
- 1 tablespoon olive oil
- 1 tablespoon chopped fresh parsley

Directions:

1. Preheat the air fryer to 180°C/360°F.
2. Season the salmon with salt and freshly ground black pepper. Then spread the Dijon mustard on the salmon, coating the entire surface.
3. Combine the breadcrumbs, horseradish, lemon zest and olive oil in a small bowl. Spread the mixture over the top of the salmon and press down lightly with your hands, adhering it to the salmon using the mustard as "glue".
4. Transfer the salmon to the air fryer basket and air-fry at 180°C/360°F for 14 minutes (depending on how thick your fillet is) or until the fish feels firm to the touch.
5. Sprinkle with the parsley.

Variations & Ingredients Tips:

- Use Dijon or whole grain mustard for a milder flavor.
- Add some grated parmesan or asiago to the breadcrumb mixture.
- Serve over a bed of sautéed spinach or roasted asparagus.

Per Serving: Calories: 400; Total Fat: 24g; Saturated Fat: 4g; Cholesterol: 85mg; Sodium: 500mg; Total Carbs: 13g; Dietary Fiber: 1g; Total Sugars: 1g; Protein: 34g

Bbq Fried Oysters

Servings: 2 | Prep Time: 10 Minutes | Cooking Time: 30 Minutes

Ingredients:

- ½ cup all-purpose flour
- ½ cup barbecue sauce
- 1 cup bread crumbs
- 225g shelled raw oysters
- 1 lemon
- 1 tbsp chopped parsley

Directions:

1. Preheat air fryer at 200°C/400°F. In a bowl, add flour. In another bowl, pour barbecue sauce and in a third bowl, add breadcrumbs.
2. Roll the oysters in the flour, shake off excess flour. Then, dip them in the sauce, shake off excess sauce. Finally, dredge them in the breadcrumbs.
3. Place oysters in the greased frying basket and Air Fry for 8 minutes, flipping once.
4. Sprinkle with parsley and squeeze lemon to serve.

Variations & Ingredients Tips:

- Use panko breadcrumbs for extra crunch.
- Add some Cajun or Old Bay seasoning to the flour.
- Serve with a spicy remoulade or Sriracha mayo dipping sauce.

Per Serving: Calories: 490; Total Fat: 13g; Saturated Fat: 2g; Cholesterol: 140mg; Sodium: 1360mg; Total Carbs: 69g; Dietary Fiber: 2g; Total Sugars: 25g; Protein: 22g

Stuffed Shrimp

Servings: 4 | Prep Time: 25 Minutes | Cooking Time: 12 Minutes Per Batch

Ingredients:

- 16 tail-on shrimp, peeled and deveined (last tail section intact)
- 3/4 cup crushed panko breadcrumbs
- Oil for misting or cooking spray
- Stuffing:
- 2 (170g) cans lump crabmeat
- 2 tablespoons chopped shallots
- 2 tablespoons chopped green onions
- 2 tablespoons chopped celery
- 2 tablespoons chopped green bell pepper
- 1/2 cup crushed saltine crackers
- 1 teaspoon Old Bay Seasoning
- 1 teaspoon garlic powder
- 1/4 teaspoon ground thyme
- 2 teaspoons dried parsley flakes
- 2 teaspoons fresh lemon juice
- 2 teaspoons Worcestershire sauce
- 1 egg, beaten

Directions:

1. Rinse shrimp. Remove tail section (shell) from 4 shrimp, discard, and chop the meat finely.
2. To prepare the remaining 12 shrimp, cut a deep slit down the back side so that the meat lies open flat. Do not cut all the way through.
3. Preheat air fryer to 180°C/360°F.
4. Place chopped shrimp in a large bowl with all of the stuffing ingredients and stir to combine.
5. Divide stuffing into 12 portions, about 2 tablespoons each.
6. Place one stuffing portion onto the back of each shrimp and form into a ball or oblong shape. Press firmly so that stuffing sticks together and adheres to shrimp.
7. Gently roll each stuffed shrimp in panko crumbs and mist with oil or cooking spray.
8. Place 6 shrimp in air fryer basket and cook at 180°C/360°F for 10 minutes. Mist with oil or spray and cook 2 minutes longer or until stuffing cooks through inside and is crispy outside.
9. Repeat step 8 to cook remaining shrimp.

Variations & Ingredients Tips:

- Substitute crab with cooked lobster, salmon or firm white fish.
- Add some diced jalapeño or red pepper flakes to the stuffing for heat.
- Serve with lemon wedges and a remoulade or cocktail sauce for dipping.

Per Serving: Calories: 290; Total Fat: 8g; Saturated Fat: 1.5g; Cholesterol: 230mg; Sodium: 940mg; Total Carbs: 19g; Dietary Fiber: 1g; Total Sugars: 2g; Protein: 34g

Masala Fish 'n' Chips

Servings: 4 | Prep Time: 15 Minutes | Cooking Time: 30 Minutes

Ingredients:

- 2 russet potatoes, cut into strips
- 4 pollock fillets
- Salt and pepper to taste
- 1/2 tsp garam masala
- 1 egg white
- 3/4 cup bread crumbs
- 2 tbsp olive oil

Directions:

1. Preheat air fryer to 200°C/400°F.
2. Sprinkle the pollock fillets with salt, pepper, and garam masala.
3. In a shallow bowl, beat egg whites until foamy. In a separate bowl, stir together bread crumbs and 1 tablespoon olive oil until completely combined.
4. Dip the fillets into the egg white, then coat with the bread crumbs.
5. In a bowl, toss the potato strips with 1 tbsp olive oil. Place them in the frying basket and Air Fry for 10 minutes.
6. Slide-out the basket, shake the chips and place a metal holder over them. Arrange the fish fillets on the metal holder and cook for 10-12 minutes, flipping once.
7. Serve warm.

Variations & Ingredients Tips:

- Use other white fish like cod or tilapia.
- Add lemon juice or other spices to the egg wash.
- Serve with malt vinegar and tartar sauce for dipping.

Per Serving: Calories: 360; Total Fat: 13g; Saturated Fat: 2g; Cholesterol: 60mg; Sodium: 430mg; Total Carbs: 38g; Dietary Fiber: 3g; Total Sugars: 2g; Protein: 23g

Southern Shrimp With Cocktail Sauce

Servings: 2 | Prep Time: 15 Minutes | Cooking Time: 20 Minutes

Ingredients:

- 225g raw shrimp, tail-on, deveined and shelled
- 1 cup ketchup
- 2 tbsp prepared horseradish
- 1 tbsp lemon juice
- 1/2 tsp Worcestershire sauce
- 1/8 tsp chili powder
- Salt and pepper to taste
- 1/3 cup flour
- 2 tbsp cornstarch
- 1/4 cup milk
- 1 egg
- 1/2 cup bread crumbs
- 1 tbsp Cajun seasoning
- 1 lemon, cut into pieces

Directions:

1. Make cocktail sauce by whisking ketchup, horseradish, lemon, Worcestershire, chili, salt and pepper. Chill until ready.
2. Preheat air fryer at 190°C/375°F.
3. In one bowl, mix flour, cornstarch and salt. In another, beat milk and egg. In third bowl, mix breadcrumbs and Cajun seasoning.
4. Dredge shrimp in flour, dip in egg, then coat in breadcrumb mixture.
5. Place shrimp in greased air fryer basket. Air Fry 8 minutes, flipping once.
6. Serve hot shrimp with chilled cocktail sauce and lemon wedges.

Variations & Ingredients Tips:

- For spicier sauce, add hot sauce or horseradish.
- Substitute panko breadcrumbs for extra crunch.
- Serve shrimp over a salad instead of as an appetizer.

Per Serving: Calories: 475; Total Fat: 9g; Saturated Fat: 2g; Cholesterol: 200mg; Sodium: 1370mg; Total Carbs: 70g; Dietary Fiber: 4g; Sugars: 16g; Protein: 28g

Lime Bay Scallops

Servings: 4 | Prep Time: 5 Minutes | Cooking Time: 10 Minutes

Ingredients:

- 2 tbsp butter, melted
- 1 lime, juiced
- 1/4 tsp salt
- 450g bay scallops
- 2 tbsp chopped cilantro

Directions:

1. Preheat air fryer to 175°C/350°F.
2. Combine butter, lime juice, salt and scallops in a bowl, except cilantro.
3. Place scallops in air fryer basket and cook for 5 minutes, tossing once.
4. Serve immediately topped with cilantro.

Variations & Ingredients Tips:

- Add minced garlic or chili flakes for extra flavor.
- Use lemon juice instead of lime if preferred.
- Serve over pasta, rice or salad greens.

Per Serving: Calories: 135; Total Fat: 6g; Saturated Fat: 3g; Cholesterol: 36mg; Sodium: 364mg; Total Carbs: 3g; Dietary Fiber: 0g; Total Sugars: 0g; Protein: 16g

Fish And "chips"

Servings: 2 | Prep Time: 15 Minutes | Cooking Time: 10 Minutes

Ingredients:

- 1/2 cup flour
- 1/2 teaspoon paprika
- 1/4 teaspoon ground white pepper (or freshly ground black pepper)
- 1 egg
- 1/4 cup mayonnaise
- 2 cups salt & vinegar kettle cooked potato chips, coarsely crushed
- 340g cod
- Tartar sauce
- Lemon wedges

Directions:

1. Set up a dredging station. Combine the flour, paprika and pepper in a shallow dish. Combine the egg and mayonnaise in a second shallow dish. Place the crushed potato chips in a third shallow dish.
2. Cut the cod into 6 pieces. Dredge each piece of fish in the flour, then dip it into the egg mixture and then place it into the crushed potato chips. Make sure all sides of the fish are covered and pat the chips gently onto the fish so they stick well.
3. Preheat the air fryer to 190°C/370°F.
4. Place the coated fish fillets into the air fry basket. (It is ok if a couple of pieces slightly overlap or rest on top of other fillets in order to fit everything in the basket.)
5. Air-fry for 10 minutes, gently turning the fish over halfway through the cooking time.
6. Transfer the fish to a platter and serve with tartar sauce and lemon wedges.

Variations & Ingredients Tips:

- Use haddock, pollack or catfish instead of cod.
- Substitute potato chips with panko breadcrumbs or crushed cornflakes.
- Serve with malt vinegar, coleslaw and mushy peas.

Per Serving: Calories: 520; Total Fat: 27g; Saturated Fat: 5g; Cholesterol: 155mg; Sodium: 570mg; Total Carbs: 35g; Dietary Fiber: 1g; Total Sugars: 1g; Protein: 35g

Horseradish Tuna Croquettes

Servings: 4 | Prep Time: 20 Minutes | Cooking Time: 40 Minutes

Ingredients:

- 1 can tuna in water, drained
- 1/3 cup mayonnaise
- 1 tbsp minced celery
- 1 green onion, sliced
- 2 tsp dried dill
- 1 tsp lime juice
- 1 cup bread crumbs
- 1 egg
- 1 tsp prepared horseradish

Directions:

1. Preheat air fryer to 190°C/370°F.
2. Add the tuna, mayonnaise, celery, green onion, dill, lime juice, 1/4 cup bread crumbs, egg, and horseradish in a bowl and mix to combine.
3. Mold the mixture into 12 rectangular mound shapes. Roll each croquette in a shallow dish with 3/4 cup of bread crumbs.
4. Place croquettes in the lightly greased frying basket and Air Fry for 12 minutes on all sides.
5. Serve.

Variations & Ingredients Tips:

- Use canned salmon or crab meat instead of tuna.
- Add some capers, lemon zest or Old Bay seasoning to the mix.
- Serve with a creamy dill sauce or tartar sauce.

Per Serving: Calories: 320; Total Fat: 20g; Saturated Fat: 3.5g; Cholesterol: 80mg; Sodium: 510mg; Total Carbs: 20g; Dietary Fiber: 1g; Total Sugars: 2g; Protein: 18g

Blackened Red Snapper

Servings: 4 | Prep Time: 5 Minutes | Cooking Time: 8 Minutes

Ingredients:

- 1 1/2 teaspoons black pepper
- 1/4 teaspoon thyme
- 1/4 teaspoon garlic powder
- 1/8 teaspoon cayenne pepper
- 1 teaspoon olive oil
- 4 (115g) red snapper fillet portions, skin on
- 4 thin slices lemon
- Cooking spray

Directions:

1. Mix the spices and oil together to make a paste. Rub into both sides of the fish.
2. Spray air fryer basket with nonstick cooking spray and lay snapper steaks in basket, skin-side down.
3. Place a lemon slice on each piece of fish.
4. Cook at 200°C/390°F for 8 minutes. The fish will not flake when done, but it should be white through the center.

Variations & Ingredients Tips:

- Use cod, tilapia or grouper instead of snapper.
- Add some smoked paprika or Old Bay seasoning to the spice mix.
- Serve with a mango salsa or avocado-lime crema.

Per Serving: Calories: 140; Total Fat: 4g; Saturated Fat: 0.5g; Cholesterol: 40mg; Sodium: 75mg; Total Carbs: 1g; Dietary Fiber: 0g; Total Sugars: 0g; Protein: 23g

Crab Cakes

Servings: 2 | Prep Time: 20 Minutes | Cooking Time: 10 Minutes

Ingredients:

- 1 teaspoon butter
- 1/3 cup finely diced onion
- 1/3 cup finely diced celery
- 1/4 cup mayonnaise
- 1 teaspoon Dijon mustard
- 1 egg
- Pinch ground cayenne pepper
- 1 teaspoon salt
- Freshly ground black pepper
- 450g lump crabmeat
- 1/2 cup + 2 tablespoons panko breadcrumbs, divided

Directions:

1. Melt the butter in a skillet over medium heat. Sauté the onion and celery until it starts to soften, but not brown – about 4 minutes. Transfer the cooked vegetables to a large bowl.
2. Add the mayonnaise, Dijon mustard, egg, cayenne pepper, salt and freshly ground black pepper to the bowl. Gently fold in the lump crabmeat and 2 tablespoons of panko breadcrumbs. Stir carefully so you don't break up all the crab pieces.
3. Preheat the air fryer to 200°C/400°F.
4. Place the remaining panko breadcrumbs in a shallow dish. Divide the crab mixture into 4 portions and shape each portion into a round patty. Dredge the crab patties in the breadcrumbs, coating both sides as well as the edges with the crumbs.
5. Air-fry the crab cakes for 5 minutes. Using a flat spatula, gently turn the cakes over and air-fry for another 5 minutes. Serve the crab cakes with tartar sauce or cocktail sauce, or dress it up with the suggestion below.

Variations & Ingredients Tips:

- Add some Old Bay seasoning or Cajun spice to the mix.
- Form into mini crab cakes and serve as an appetizer.
- Top with a lemon-herb aioli or spicy remoulade.

Per Serving: Calories: 420; Total Fat: 24g; Saturated Fat: 5g; Cholesterol: 275mg; Sodium: 1720mg; Total Carbs: 21g; Dietary Fiber: 1g; Total Sugars: 3g; Protein: 32g

Catalan-style Crab Samfaina

Servings: 4 | Prep Time: 15 Minutes | Cooking Time: 30 Minutes

Ingredients:

- 1 peeled eggplant, cubed
- 1 zucchini, cubed
- 1 onion, chopped
- 1 red bell pepper, chopped
- 2 large tomatoes, chopped
- 1 tbsp olive oil
- ½ tsp dried thyme
- ½ tsp dried basil
- Salt and pepper to taste
- 1 ½ cups cooked crab meat

Directions:

1. Preheat air fryer to 200°C/400°F.
2. In a pan, mix together all ingredients, except the crabmeat. Place the pan in the air fryer and Bake for 9 minutes.
3. Remove the bowl and stir in the crabmeat. Return to the air fryer and roast for another 2-5 minutes until the vegetables are tender and ratatouille bubbling.
4. Serve hot.

Variations & Ingredients Tips:

- Use canned or fresh lump crab meat, or substitute with cooked shrimp or lobster.
- Add minced garlic, capers, or olives for extra Mediterranean flavors.
- Serve with crusty bread, rice, or pasta to soak up the juices.

Per Serving: Calories: 160; Total Fat: 6g; Saturated Fat: 1g; Sodium: 430mg; Total Carbohydrates: 14g; Dietary Fiber: 5g; Total Sugars: 8g; Protein: 14g

Fish Sticks With Tartar Sauce

Servings: 2 | Prep Time: 15 Minutes | Cooking Time: 6 Minutes

Ingredients:

- 340g cod or flounder
- 1/2 cup flour
- 1/2 teaspoon paprika
- 1 teaspoon salt
- Freshly ground black pepper
- 2 eggs, lightly beaten
- 1 1/2 cups panko breadcrumbs
- 1 teaspoon salt
- Vegetable oil
- Tartar Sauce:
- 1/4 cup mayonnaise
- 2 teaspoons lemon juice
- 2 tablespoons finely chopped sweet pickles
- Salt and pepper

Directions:

1. Cut fish into 2cm wide sticks. Set up 3 dishes: flour+spices, eggs, and breadcrumbs+salt.
2. Coat fish in flour, egg, then breadcrumbs, pressing to adhere.
3. Preheat air fryer to 200°C/400°F. Spray fish with oil.
4. Air fry for 4 mins, flip and cook 2 more mins.
5. Make tartar sauce by mixing ingredients.
6. Serve fish sticks warm with tartar sauce.

Variations & Ingredients Tips:

- Add Old Bay or cajun seasoning to the breadcrumb mix.
- Bake instead of air frying at 400°F for 12-15 mins.
- Serve with lemon wedges, malt vinegar or rémoulade sauce.

Per Serving: Calories: 469; Total Fat: 17g; Saturated Fat: 3g; Cholesterol: 202mg; Sodium: 1710mg; Total Carbs: 48g; Dietary Fiber: 2g; Total Sugars: 2g; Protein: 30g

Tilapia Teriyaki

Servings: 3 | Prep Time: 10 Minutes | Cooking Time: 10 Minutes

Ingredients:

- 4 tablespoons teriyaki sauce
- 1 tablespoon pineapple juice
- 450g tilapia fillets
- Cooking spray
- 170g frozen mixed peppers with onions, thawed and drained
- 2 cups cooked rice

Directions:

1. Mix the teriyaki sauce and pineapple juice together in a small bowl.
2. Split tilapia fillets down the center lengthwise.
3. Brush all sides of fish with the sauce, spray air fryer basket with nonstick cooking spray, and place fish in the basket.
4. Stir the peppers and onions into the remaining sauce and spoon over the fish. Save any leftover sauce for drizzling over the fish when serving.
5. Cook at 180°C/360°F for 10 minutes, until fish flakes easily with a fork and is done in center.
6. Divide into 3 or 4 servings and serve each with approximately 120ml/1/2 cup cooked rice.

Variations & Ingredients Tips:

- Use salmon, cod or halibut instead of tilapia.
- Add some diced pineapple or mango to the veggies.
- Sprinkle with toasted sesame seeds and sliced scallions before serving.

Per Serving: Calories: 290; Total Fat: 4g; Saturated Fat: 1g; Cholesterol: 85mg; Sodium: 810mg; Total Carbs: 34g; Dietary Fiber: 2g; Total Sugars: 9g; Protein: 30g

Black Cod With Grapes, Fennel, Pecans And Kale

Servings: 2 | Prep Time: 10 Minutes | Cooking Time: 15 Minutes

Ingredients:

- 2 (170-225g) fillets of black cod (or sablefish)
- Salt and freshly ground black pepper
- Olive oil
- 1 cup grapes, halved
- 1 small bulb fennel, sliced 6-mm thick
- ½ cup pecans
- 3 cups shredded kale
- 2 teaspoons white balsamic vinegar or white wine vinegar
- 2 tablespoons extra virgin olive oil

Directions:

1. Preheat the air fryer to 200°C/400°F.
2. Season the cod fillets with salt and pepper and drizzle, brush or spray a little olive oil on top. Place the fish, presentation side up (skin side down), into the air fryer basket. Air-fry for 10 minutes.
3. When the fish has finished cooking, remove the fillets to a side plate and loosely tent with foil to rest.
4. Toss the grapes, fennel and pecans in a bowl with a drizzle of olive oil and season with salt and pepper. Add the grapes, fennel and pecans to the air fryer basket and air-fry for 5 minutes at 200°C/400°F, shaking the basket once during the cooking time.
5. Transfer the grapes, fennel and pecans to a bowl with the kale. Dress the kale with the balsamic vinegar and olive oil, season to taste with salt and pepper and serve along side the cooked fish.

Variations & Ingredients Tips:

- Use salmon, halibut or sea bass instead of black cod.
- Substitute grapes with sliced apples or pears.
- Toast the pecans before air frying for extra nuttiness.

Per Serving: Calories: 540; Total Fat: 35g; Saturated Fat: 5g; Cholesterol: 100mg; Sodium: 370mg; Total Carbs: 24g; Dietary Fiber: 6g; Total Sugars: 14g; Protein: 38g

Beer-breaded Halibut Fish Tacos

Servings: 4 | Prep Time: 40 Minutes | Cooking Time: 10 Minutes

Ingredients:

- 450g halibut, cut into 2.5-cm strips
- 1 cup light beer
- 1 jalapeño, minced and divided
- 1 clove garlic, minced
- 1/4 teaspoon ground cumin
- ½ cup cornmeal
- ¼ cup all-purpose flour
- 1¼ teaspoons sea salt, divided
- 2 cups shredded cabbage
- 1 lime, juiced and divided
- ¼ cup Greek yogurt
- ¼ cup Greek yogurt
- 1 cup grape tomatoes, quartered
- ½ cup chopped cilantro
- ¼ cup chopped onion
- 1 egg, whisked
- 8 corn tortillas

Directions:

1. In a shallow baking dish, place the fish, the beer, 1 teaspoon of the minced jalapeño, the garlic, and the cumin. Cover and refrigerate for 30 minutes.
2. Meanwhile, in a medium bowl, mix together the cornmeal, flour, and 1/2 teaspoon of the salt.
3. In large bowl, mix together the shredded cabbage, 1 tablespoon of the lime juice, the Greek yogurt, the mayonnaise, and 1/2 teaspoon of the salt.
4. In a small bowl, make the pico de gallo by mixing together the tomatoes, cilantro, onion, 1/4 teaspoon of the salt, the remaining jalapeño, and the remaining lime juice.

5. Remove the fish from the refrigerator and discard the marinade. Dredge the fish in the whisked egg; then dredge the fish in the cornmeal flour mixture, until all pieces of fish have been breaded.
6. Preheat the air fryer to 175°C/350°F.
7. Place the fish in the air fryer basket and spray liberally with cooking spray. Cook for 6 minutes, flip and shake the fish, and cook another 4 minutes.
8. While the fish is cooking, heat the tortillas in a heavy skillet for 1 to 2 minutes over high heat.
9. To assemble the tacos, place the battered fish on the heated tortillas, and top with slaw and pico de gallo. Serve immediately.

Variations & Ingredients Tips:

- Use cod, tilapia or snapper instead of halibut.
- Substitute the beer with sparkling water or ginger ale for a non-alcoholic version.
- Add some sliced avocado or guacamole on top.

Per Serving: Calories: 420; Total Fat: 18g; Saturated Fat: 4g; Cholesterol: 120mg; Sodium: 910mg; Total Carbs: 37g; Dietary Fiber: 5g; Total Sugars: 5g; Protein: 29g

Crispy Sweet-and-sour Cod Fillets

Servings: 3 | Prep Time: 10 Minutes | Cooking Time: 12 Minutes

Ingredients:

- 1 1/2 cups plain panko bread crumbs (gluten-free, if a concern)
- 2 tablespoons regular or low-fat mayonnaise (not fat-free; gluten-free, if a concern)
- 1/4 cup sweet pickle relish
- 3 (115to 140g) skinless cod fillets

Directions:

1. Preheat the air fryer to 200°C/400°F.
2. Pour the bread crumbs into a shallow soup plate or a small pie plate.
3. Mix the mayonnaise and relish in a small bowl until well combined. Smear this mixture all over the cod fillets. Set them in the crumbs and turn until evenly coated on all sides, even on the ends.
4. Set the coated cod fillets in the basket with as much air space between them as possible. They should not touch. Air-fry undisturbed for 12 minutes, or until browned and crisp.
5. Use a nonstick-safe spatula to transfer the cod pieces to a wire rack. Cool for only a minute or two before serving hot.

Variations & Ingredients Tips:

- Use tilapia, basa or catfish instead of cod.
- Substitute pickle relish with sweet chili sauce or mango chutney.
- Sprinkle with chopped scallions and toasted sesame seeds before serving.

Per Serving: Calories: 280; Total Fat: 8g; Saturated Fat: 1.5g; Cholesterol: 85mg; Sodium: 630mg; Total Carbs: 24g; Dietary Fiber: 1g; Total Sugars: 5g; Protein: 27g

Catfish Nuggets

Servings: 4 | Prep Time: 15 Minutes | Cooking Time: 7 Minutes Per Batch

Ingredients:

- 2 medium catfish fillets, cut in chunks (approximately 2.5 x 5 cm)
- salt and pepper
- 2 eggs
- 2 tablespoons skim milk
- ½ cup cornstarch
- 1 cup panko breadcrumbs, crushed
- oil for misting or cooking spray

Directions:

1. Season catfish chunks with salt and pepper to your liking.
2. Beat together eggs and milk in a small bowl.
3. Place cornstarch in a second small bowl.
4. Place breadcrumbs in a third small bowl.
5. Dip catfish chunks in cornstarch, dip in egg wash, shake off excess, then roll in breadcrumbs.
6. Spray all sides of catfish chunks with oil or cooking spray.
7. Place chunks in air fryer basket in a single layer, leaving space between for air circulation.
8. Cook at 200°C/390°F for 4 minutes, turn, and cook an additional 3 minutes, until fish flakes easily and outside is crispy brown.
9. Repeat steps 7 and 8 to cook remaining catfish nuggets.

Variations & Ingredients Tips:

- Use cod, tilapia, or halibut instead of catfish for different fish options.
- Add garlic powder, onion powder, or Old Bay seasoning to the breading mix for extra flavor.
- Serve with tartar sauce, remoulade, or cocktail sauce for dipping.

Per Serving: Calories: 280; Total Fat: 9g; Saturated Fat: 2g; Sodium: 420mg; Total Carbohydrates: 25g; Dietary Fiber: 1g; Total Sugars: 2g; Protein: 24g

French Grouper Nicoise

Servings: 4 | Prep Time: 10 Minutes | Cooking Time: 20 Minutes

Ingredients:

- 4 grouper fillets
- Salt to taste

- 1/2 tsp ground cumin
- 3 garlic cloves, minced
- 1 tomato, sliced
- 1/4 cup sliced Nicoise olives
- 1/4 cup dill, chopped
- 1 lemon, juiced
- 1/4 cup olive oil

Directions:

1. Preheat air fryer to 195°C/380°F.
2. Season grouper fillets with salt and cumin.
3. Arrange fillets in greased air fryer basket.
4. Top with garlic, tomato, olives and fresh dill.
5. Drizzle with lemon juice and olive oil.
6. Bake for 10-12 minutes.
7. Serve and enjoy!

Variations & Ingredients Tips:

- Use other white fish like halibut or cod.
- Add capers, red onion or roasted red peppers.
- Serve over arugula or with roasted potatoes.

Per Serving: Calories: 275; Total Fat: 13g; Saturated Fat: 2g; Cholesterol: 86mg; Sodium: 267mg; Total Carbs: 3g; Dietary Fiber: 1g; Total Sugars: 0g; Protein: 35g

Chili Blackened Shrimp

Servings: 4 | Prep Time: 5 Minutes | Cooking Time: 15 Minutes

Ingredients:

- 454 grams peeled shrimp, deveined
- 1 tsp paprika
- ½ tsp dried dill
- ½ tsp red chili flakes
- ½ lemon, juiced
- Salt and pepper to taste

Directions:

1. Preheat air fryer to 200°C/400°F.
2. In a resealable bag, add shrimp, paprika, dill, red chili flakes, lemon juice, salt and pepper. Seal and shake well.
3. Place the shrimp in the greased air fryer basket and Air Fry for 7-8 minutes, shaking the basket once until blackened.
4. Let cool slightly and serve.

Variations & Ingredients Tips:

- Add minced garlic, onion powder, or cumin to the seasoning mix for extra flavor.
- Serve over rice, quinoa, or in tacos, salads, or pasta dishes.
- Brush with melted butter or olive oil before air frying for extra richness.

Per Serving: Calories: 120; Total Fat: 1.5g; Saturated Fat: 0g; Sodium: 180mg; Total Carbohydrates: 2g; Dietary Fiber: 0g; Total Sugars: 0g; Protein: 23g

Beer-battered Cod

Servings: 3 | Prep Time: 15 Minutes | Cooking Time: 12 Minutes

Ingredients:

- 1½ cups All-purpose flour
- 3 tablespoons Old Bay seasoning
- 1 large egg
- ¼ cup Amber beer, pale ale, or IPA
- 3 (115g) skinless cod fillets
- Vegetable oil spray

Directions:

1. Preheat the air fryer to 200°C/400°F.
2. Set up and fill two shallow soup plates or small pie plates on your counter: one with the flour, whisked with the Old Bay until well combined; and one with the egg, whisked with the beer until foamy and uniform.
3. Dip a piece of cod in the flour mixture, turning it to coat on all sides (not just the top and bottom). Gently shake off any excess flour and dip the fish in the egg mixture, turning it to coat. Let any excess egg mixture slip back into the rest, then set the fish back in the flour mixture and coat it again, then back in the egg mixture for a second wash, then back in the flour mixture for a third time. Coat the fish on all sides with vegetable oil spray and set it aside. "Batter" the remaining piece(s) of cod in the same way.
4. Set the coated cod fillets in the basket with as much space between them as possible. They should not touch. Air-fry undisturbed for 12 minutes, or until brown and crisp.
5. Use kitchen tongs to gently transfer the fish to a wire rack. Cool for only a couple of minutes before serving.

Variations & Ingredients Tips:

- Use haddock, pollack or catfish instead of cod.
- Substitute beer with sparkling water for a non-alcoholic version.
- Serve with french fries, coleslaw and malt vinegar.

Per Serving: Calories: 330; Total Fat: 5g; Saturated Fat: 1g; Cholesterol: 115mg; Sodium: 1120mg; Total Carbs: 44g; Dietary Fiber: 2g; Total Sugars: 1g; Protein: 26g

Sriracha Salmon Melt Sandwiches

Servings: 4 | Prep Time: 10 Minutes | Cooking Time: 20 Minutes

Ingredients:

- 2 tbsp butter, softened
- 2 (210g) cans pink salmon
- 2 English muffins
- 1/3 cup mayonnaise
- 2 tbsp Dijon mustard
- 1 tbsp fresh lemon juice
- 1/3 cup chopped celery
- 1/2 tsp sriracha sauce
- 4 slices tomato
- 4 slices Swiss cheese

Directions:

1. Preheat air fryer to 190°C/370°F.
2. Split muffins and spread with butter. Toast in air fryer 3-5 mins until golden.
3. Mix salmon, mayo, mustard, lemon, celery and sriracha.
4. Top muffin halves with salmon mixture, tomato and cheese.
5. Air fry sandwiches 4-6 minutes until cheese melts.
6. Serve hot.

Variations & Ingredients Tips:

- Use canned tuna or crab meat instead of salmon.
- Add diced onion, pickles or jalapeño to the filling.
- Brush muffins with garlic butter before toasting.

Per Serving: Calories: 430; Total Fat: 30g; Saturated Fat: 10g; Cholesterol: 95mg; Sodium: 780mg; Total Carbs: 18g; Dietary Fiber: 2g; Sugars: 4g; Protein: 23g

Coconut Jerk Shrimp

Servings: 3 | Prep Time: 10 Minutes | Cooking Time: 8 Minutes

Ingredients:

- 1 Large egg white
- 1 teaspoon Purchased or homemade jerk dried seasoning blend
- 3/4 cup Plain panko bread crumbs (gluten-free, if a concern)
- 3/4 cup Unsweetened shredded coconut
- 12 Large shrimp (20-25 per gram), peeled and deveined
- Coconut oil spray

Directions:

1. Preheat the air fryer to 190°C/375°F.
2. Whisk the egg white and seasoning blend in a bowl until foamy. Add the shrimp and toss well to coat evenly.
3. Mix the bread crumbs and coconut on a dinner plate until well combined. Use kitchen tongs to pick up a shrimp, letting the excess egg white mixture slip back into the rest. Set the shrimp in the bread-crumb mixture. Turn several times to coat evenly and thoroughly. Set on a cutting board and continue coating the remainder of the shrimp.
4. Lightly coat all the shrimp on both sides with the coconut oil spray. Set them in the basket in one layer with as much space between them as possible. (You can even stand some up along the basket's wall in some models.)
5. Air-fry undisturbed for 6 minutes, or until the coating is lightly browned. If the air fryer is at 180°C/360°F, you may need to add 2 minutes to the cooking time.
6. Use clean kitchen tongs to transfer the shrimp to a wire rack. Cool for only a minute or two before serving.

Variations & Ingredients Tips:

- Use gluten-free breadcrumbs if needed.
- Adjust jerk seasoning amount to taste preference.
- Serve with a lime wedge and dipping sauce like pineapple salsa or mango chutney.

Per Serving: Calories: 240; Total Fat: 12g; Saturated Fat: 8g; Cholesterol: 145mg; Sodium: 420mg; Total Carbs: 18g; Dietary Fiber: 2g; Total Sugars: 3g; Protein: 15g

Coconut Shrimp With Plum Sauce

Servings: 2 | Prep Time: 15 Minutes | Cooking Time: 30 Minutes

Ingredients:

- 225g raw shrimp, peeled
- 2 eggs
- 1/2 cup breadcrumbs
- 1 tsp red chili powder
- 2 tbsp dried coconut flakes
- Salt and pepper to taste
- 1/2 cup plum sauce

Directions:

1. Preheat air fryer to 180°C/350°F.
2. Whisk the eggs with salt and pepper in a bowl. Dip in the shrimp, fully submerging.
3. Combine the bread crumbs, coconut flakes, chili powder, salt, and pepper in another bowl until evenly blended.
4. Coat the shrimp in the crumb mixture and place them in the foil-lined frying basket.
5. Air Fry for 14-16 minutes. Halfway through the cooking time, shake the basket.
6. Serve with plum sauce for dipping and enjoy!

Variations & Ingredients Tips:

- Use panko breadcrumbs for an extra crispy coating.
- Add garlic powder or cajun seasoning to the breading.
- Serve with a sweet chili dipping sauce instead of plum sauce.

Per Serving: Calories: 287; Total Fat: 5g; Saturated Fat: 2g; Cholesterol: 204mg; Sodium: 915mg; Total Carbs: 35g; Dietary Fiber: 2g; Total Sugars: 10g; Protein: 26g

Beef, Pork & Lamb Recipes

Korean-style Lamb Shoulder Chops

Servings: 3 | Prep Time: 15 Minutes | Cooking Time: 28 Minutes

Ingredients:

- ⅓ cup Regular or low-sodium soy sauce or gluten-free tamari sauce
- 1½ tablespoons Toasted sesame oil
- 1½ tablespoons Granulated white sugar
- 2 teaspoons Minced peeled fresh ginger
- 1 teaspoon Minced garlic
- ¼ teaspoon Red pepper flakes
- 3 170g bone-in lamb shoulder chops, any excess fat trimmed
- ⅔ cup Tapioca flour
- Vegetable oil spray

Directions:

1. Put the soy or tamari sauce, sesame oil, sugar, ginger, garlic, and red pepper flakes in a large, heavy zip-closed plastic bag. Add the chops, seal, and rub the marinade evenly over them through the bag. Refrigerate for at least 2 hours or up to 6 hours, turning the bag at least once so the chops move around in the marinade.
2. Set the bag out on the counter as the air fryer heats. Preheat the air fryer to 375°F/191°C.
3. Pour the tapioca flour on a dinner plate or in a small pie plate. Remove a chop from the marinade and dredge it on both sides in the tapioca flour, coating it evenly and well. Coat both sides with vegetable oil spray, set it in the basket, and dredge and spray the remaining chop(s), setting them in the basket in a single layer with space between them. Discard the bag with the marinade.
4. Air-fry, turning once, for 25 minutes, or until the chops are well browned and tender when pierced with the point of a paring knife. If the machine is at 360°F/182°C, you may need to add up to 3 minutes to the cooking time.
5. Use kitchen tongs to transfer the chops to a wire rack. Cool for just a couple of minutes before serving.

Variations & Ingredients Tips:

- Use lamb loin chops instead of shoulder for a leaner cut
- Add grated orange zest or juice to the marinade
- Serve with kimchi and steamed rice on the side

Per Serving: Calories: 410; Total Fat: 23g; Saturated Fat: 7g; Cholesterol: 90mg; Sodium: 1340mg; Total Carbs: 19g; Dietary Fiber: 1g; Total Sugars: 6g; Protein: 31g

Calf's Liver

Servings: 4 | Prep Time: 10 Minutes | Cooking Time: 5 Minutes

Ingredients:

- 450-g sliced calf's liver
- Salt and pepper
- 2 eggs
- 2 tablespoons milk
- 1/2 cup whole wheat flour
- 1 1/2 cups panko breadcrumbs
- 1/2 cup plain breadcrumbs
- 1/2 teaspoon salt
- 1/4 teaspoon pepper
- Oil for misting or cooking spray

Directions:

1. Cut liver slices crosswise into strips about 25cm wide. Sprinkle with salt and pepper to taste.
2. Beat together egg and milk in a shallow dish.
3. Place wheat flour in a second shallow dish.
4. In a third shallow dish, mix together panko, plain breadcrumbs, 1/2 teaspoon salt, and 1/4 teaspoon pepper.
5. Preheat air fryer to 390°F/199°C.
6. Dip liver strips in flour, egg wash, and then breadcrumbs, pressing in coating slightly to make crumbs stick.
7. Cooking half the liver at a time, place strips in air fryer basket in a single layer, close but not touching. Cook at 390°F/199°C for 5 minutes or until done to your preference.
8. Repeat step 7 to cook remaining liver.

Variations & Ingredients Tips:

- For extra crunch, use all panko breadcrumbs instead of a mix
- Add cayenne pepper or Cajun seasoning to the breadcrumb mix for a kick of flavor
- Serve with lemon wedges for squeezing over the cooked liver

Per Serving: Calories: 276; Total Fat: 8g; Saturated Fat: 2g; Cholesterol: 284mg; Sodium: 620mg; Total Carbs: 27g; Dietary Fiber: 2g; Total Sugars: 1g; Protein: 23g

Perfect Strip Steaks

Servings: 2 | Prep Time: 5 Minutes | Cooking Time: 17 Minutes

Ingredients:

- 1½ tablespoons olive oil
- 1½ tablespoons minced

- garlic
- 2 teaspoons ground black pepper
- 1 teaspoon table salt
- 2 boneless beef strip steaks (340 g each)

Directions:

1. Preheat the air fryer to 190°C/375°F (or 200°C/380°F or 200°C/390°F, if one of these is the closest setting).
2. Mix the oil, garlic, pepper, and salt in a small bowl, then smear this mixture over both sides of the steak(s).
3. When the machine is at temperature, put the steak(s) in the basket with as much air space as possible between them for the larger batch. They should not overlap or even touch. That said, even just a 6 mm between them will work. Air-fry for 12 minutes, turning once, until an instant-read meat thermometer inserted into the thickest part of a steak registers 55°C/127°F for rare (not USDA-approved). Or air-fry for 15 minutes, turning once, until an instant-read meat thermometer registers 65°C/145°F for medium (USDA-approved). If the machine is at 200°C/390°F, the steaks may cook 2 minutes more quickly than the stated timing.
4. Use kitchen tongs to transfer the steak(s) to a wire rack. Cool for 5 minutes before serving.

Variations & Ingredients Tips:

- Use different types of seasoning, such as steak seasoning or chimichurri, for a variety of flavors.
- Add some sliced onions or mushrooms to the steak for extra flavor and texture.
- Serve the strip steaks with a side of roasted potatoes or a Caesar salad for a classic steakhouse meal.

Per Serving: Calories: 690; Total Fat: 51g; Saturated Fat: 17g; Cholesterol: 170mg; Sodium: 1180mg; Total Carbs: 2g; Fiber: 0g; Sugars: 0g; Protein: 52g

Barbecue-style London Broil

Servings: 5 | Prep Time: 5 Minutes | Cooking Time: 17 Minutes

Ingredients:

- ¾ tsp mild smoked paprika
- ¾ tsp dried oregano
- ¾ tsp table salt
- ¾ tsp ground black pepper
- ¼ tsp garlic powder
- ¼ tsp onion powder
- 680 g beef London broil (in one piece)
- Olive oil spray

Directions:

1. Preheat the air fryer to 200°C/400°F. Mix the smoked paprika, oregano, salt, pepper, garlic powder, and onion powder in a small bowl until uniform. Pat and rub this mixture across all surfaces of the beef. Lightly coat the beef on all sides with olive oil spray. When the machine is at temperature, lay the London broil flat in the basket and air-fry undisturbed for 8 minutes for the small batch, 10 minutes for the medium batch, or 12 minutes for the large batch for medium-rare, until an instant-read meat thermometer inserted into the center of the meat registers 55°C/130°F (not USDA-approved). Add 1, 2, or 3 minutes, respectively (based on the size of the cut) for medium, until an instant-read meat thermometer registers 57°C/135°F (not USDA-approved). Or add 3, 4, or 5 minutes respectively for medium, until an instant-read meat thermometer registers 63°C/145°F (USDA-approved). Use kitchen tongs to transfer the London broil to a cutting board. Let the meat rest for 10 minutes. It needs a long time for the juices to be reincorporated into the meat's fibers. Carve it against the grain into very thin (less than 6-mm-thick) slices to serve.

Variations & Ingredients Tips:

- Marinate the beef in a mixture of soy sauce, Worcestershire sauce, olive oil, and garlic for extra flavor.
- Slice the cooked London broil and serve in sandwiches, salads, or wraps.
- Brush with chimichurri sauce or horseradish cream sauce before serving for a bright, tangy finish.

Per Serving: Calories: 213; Total Fat: 10g; Saturated Fat: 4g; Cholesterol: 74mg; Sodium: 416mg; Total Carbohydrates: 1g; Dietary Fiber: 0g; Total Sugars: 0g; Protein: 28g

Grilled Pork & Bell Pepper Salad

Servings: 4 | Prep Time: 15 Minutes | Cooking Time: 25 Minutes

Ingredients:

- 1 cup sautéed button mushrooms, sliced
- 907 g pork tenderloin, sliced
- 1 tsp olive oil
- 1 tsp dried marjoram
- 6 tomato wedges
- 6 green olives
- 6 cups mixed salad greens
- 1 red bell pepper, sliced
- 1/3 cup vinaigrette dressing

Directions:

1. Preheat air fryer to 200°C/400°F. Combine the pork and olive oil, making sure the pork is well-coated. Season with marjoram. Lay the pork in the air fryer. Grill for 4-6 minutes, turning once until the pork is cooked through.
2. While the pork is cooking, toss the salad greens, red bell pepper, tomatoes, olives, and mushrooms into a bowl. Lay the pork slices on top of the salad, season with vinaigrette, and toss. Serve while the pork is still warm.

Variations & Ingredients Tips:

- Add some crumbled feta or goat cheese for a creamy tang
- Use baby spinach or arugula instead of mixed greens for a peppery kick
- Grill some red onion slices along with the pork for extra flavor

Per Serving: Calories: 405; Total Fat: 18g; Saturated Fat: 4g; Cholesterol: 147mg; Sodium: 289mg; Total Carbs: 8g; Dietary Fiber: 3g; Total Sugars: 4g; Protein: 53g

Greek Pork Chops

Servings: 4 | Prep Time: 10 Minutes | Cooking Time: 30 Minutes

Ingredients:

- 3 tbsp grated Halloumi cheese
- 4 pork chops
- 1 tsp Greek seasoning
- Salt and pepper to taste
- ¼ cup all-purpose flour
- 2 tbsp bread crumbs

Directions:

1. Preheat air fryer to 190°C/380°F. Season the pork chops with Greek seasoning, salt and pepper. In a shallow bowl, add flour. In another shallow bowl, combine the crumbs and Halloumi. Dip the chops in the flour, then in the bread crumbs. Place them in the fryer and spray with cooking oil. Bake for 12-14 minutes, flipping once. Serve warm.

Variations & Ingredients Tips:

- Use feta cheese instead of Halloumi for a tangier flavor
- Add some dried herbs like oregano or thyme to the breading mixture
- Serve with a Greek salad and lemon potatoes

Per Serving: Calories: 277; Total Fat: 14g; Saturated Fat: 6g; Cholesterol: 80mg; Sodium: 417mg; Total Carbs: 10g; Dietary Fiber: 0g; Total Sugars: 0g; Protein: 28g

Tamari-seasoned Pork Strips

Servings: 4 | Prep Time: 10 Minutes | Cooking Time: 40 Minutes

Ingredients:

- 3 tablespoons olive oil
- 2 tablespoons tamari
- 2 teaspoons red chili paste
- 2 teaspoons yellow mustard
- 2 teaspoons granulated sugar
- 454 g pork shoulder strips
- 1 cup white rice, cooked
- 6 scallions, chopped
- ½ teaspoon garlic powder
- 1 tablespoon lemon juice
- 1 teaspoon lemon zest
- ½ teaspoon salt

Directions:

1. Add 2 tbsp of olive oil, tamari, chili paste, mustard, and sugar to a bowl and whisk until everything is well mixed. Set aside half of the marinade. Toss pork strips in the remaining marinade and put in the fridge for 30 minutes.
2. Preheat air fryer to 175°C/350°F. Place the pork strips in the frying basket and Air Fry for 16-18 minutes, tossing once. Transfer cooked pork to the bowl along with the remaining marinade and toss to coat. Set aside. In a medium bowl, stir in the cooked rice, garlic, lemon juice, lemon zest, and salt and cover. Spread on a serving plate. Arrange the pork strips over and top with scallions. Serve.

Variations & Ingredients Tips:

- Use chicken thighs or beef sirloin instead of pork
- Substitute tamari with soy sauce or coconut aminos
- Serve over cauliflower rice or zucchini noodles for low-carb

Per Serving: Calories: 466; Total Fat: 27g; Saturated Fat: 6g; Cholesterol: 100mg; Sodium: 998mg; Total Carbs: 28g; Dietary Fiber: 1g; Total Sugars: 3g; Protein: 31g

Wasabi Pork Medallions

Servings: 4 | Prep Time: 10 Minutes | Cooking Time: 20 Minutes

Ingredients:

- 454g pork medallions
- 1 cup soy sauce
- 1 tbsp mirin
- 1/2 cup olive oil
- 3 cloves garlic, crushed
- 1 tsp fresh grated ginger
- 1 tsp wasabi paste
- 1 tbsp brown sugar

Directions:

1. Place all ingredients, except for the pork, in a resealable bag and shake to combine. Add the pork medallions to the bag, shake again, and place in the fridge to marinate for 2 hours. Preheat air fryer to 360°F/182°C. Remove pork medallions from the marinade and place them in the frying basket in rows. Air Fry for 14-16 minutes or until the medallions are cooked through and juicy. Serve.

Variations & Ingredients Tips:

- Use pork tenderloin instead of medallions and slice into medallions after cooking
- Add sliced green onions or sesame seeds as a garnish
- Substitute rice vinegar for the mirin for a different flavor

Per Serving: Calories: 430; Total Fat: 25g; Saturated Fat: 6g; Cholesterol: 90mg; Sodium: 2850mg; Total Carbs: 13g; Dietary Fiber: 1g; Total Sugars: 6g; Protein: 35g

Delicious Juicy Pork Meatballs

Servings: 4 | Prep Time: 10 Minutes | Cooking Time: 35 Minutes

Ingredients:

- ¼ cup grated cheddar cheese
- 450 g ground pork
- 1 egg

- 1 tablespoon Greek yogurt
- ½ teaspoon onion powder
- ¼ cup chopped parsley
- 2 tablespoons bread crumbs
- ¼ teaspoon garlic powder
- Salt and pepper to taste

Directions:

1. Preheat air fryer to 180°C/350°F.
2. In a bowl, combine the ground pork, egg, yogurt, onion, parsley, cheddar cheese, bread crumbs, garlic, salt, and black pepper. Form mixture into 16 meatballs.
3. Place meatballs in the lightly greased frying basket and Air Fry for 8-10 minutes, flipping once.
4. Serve.

Variations & Ingredients Tips:

- Use different types of cheese, such as mozzarella or Parmesan, for a variety of flavors.
- Add some minced jalapeño or red pepper flakes to the meatball mixture for a spicy kick.
- Serve the meatballs with a side of tomato sauce or barbecue sauce for dipping.

Per Serving: Calories: 320; Total Fat: 22g; Saturated Fat: 9g; Cholesterol: 135mg; Sodium: 280mg; Total Carbs: 5g; Fiber: 0g; Sugars: 1g; Protein: 27g

Pepper Steak

Servings: 4 | Prep Time: 40 Minutes | Cooking Time: 30 Minutes

Ingredients:

- 2 tablespoons cornstarch
- 1 tablespoon sugar
- ¾ cup beef broth
- ¼ cup hoisin sauce
- 3 tablespoons soy sauce
- 1 teaspoon sesame oil
- ½ teaspoon freshly ground black pepper
- 680 g boneless New York strip steaks, sliced into 1.25 cm strips
- 1 onion, sliced
- 3 small bell peppers, red, yellow and green, sliced

Directions:

1. Whisk the cornstarch and sugar together in a large bowl to break up any lumps in the cornstarch. Add the beef broth and whisk until combined and smooth. Stir in the hoisin sauce, soy sauce, sesame oil and freshly ground black pepper.
2. Add the beef, onion and peppers, and toss to coat. Marinate the beef and vegetables at room temperature for 30 minutes, stirring a few times to keep meat and vegetables coated.
3. Preheat the air fryer to 180°C/350°F.
4. Transfer the beef, onion, and peppers to the air fryer basket with tongs, reserving the marinade. Air-fry the beef and vegetables for 30 minutes, stirring well two or three times during the cooking process.
5. While the beef is air-frying, bring the reserved marinade to a simmer in a small saucepan over medium heat on the stovetop. Simmer for 5 minutes until the sauce thickens.
6. When the steak and vegetables have finished cooking, transfer them to a serving platter. Pour the hot sauce over the pepper steak and serve with white rice.

Variations & Ingredients Tips:

- Use different types of steak, such as sirloin or flank steak, for a variety of flavors and textures.
- Add some sliced mushrooms or water chestnuts to the beef and vegetable mixture for extra texture.
- Serve the pepper steak with a side of steamed broccoli or bok choy for a complete Chinese-inspired meal.

Per Serving: Calories: 410; Total Fat: 18g; Saturated Fat: 6g; Cholesterol: 100mg; Sodium: 1320mg; Total Carbs: 22g; Fiber: 3g; Sugars: 11g; Protein: 41g

Italian Sausage & Peppers

Servings: 6 | Prep Time: 20 Minutes | Cooking Time: 25 Minutes

Ingredients:

- 1 170g can tomato paste
- 2/3 cup water
- 1 225g can tomato sauce
- 1 teaspoon dried parsley flakes
- 1/2 teaspoon garlic powder
- 1/8 teaspoon oregano
- 225g mild Italian bulk sausage
- 1 tablespoon extra virgin olive oil
- 1/2 large onion, cut in 2.5cm chunks
- 113g fresh mushrooms, sliced
- 1 large green bell pepper, cut in 2.5cm chunks
- 227g spaghetti, cooked
- Parmesan cheese for serving

Directions:

1. In a large saucepan or skillet, stir together the tomato paste, water, tomato sauce, parsley, garlic, and oregano. Heat on stovetop over very low heat while preparing meat and vegetables.
2. Break sausage into small chunks, about 1.25cm pieces. Place in air fryer baking pan.
3. Cook at 390°F/199°C for 5 minutes. Stir. Cook 7 minutes longer or until sausage is well done. Remove from pan, drain on paper towels, and add to the sauce mixture.
4. If any sausage grease remains in baking pan, pour it off or use paper towels to soak it up. (Be careful handling that hot pan!)
5. Place olive oil, onions, and mushrooms in pan and stir. Cook for 5 minutes or just until tender. Using a slotted spoon, transfer onions and mushrooms from baking pan into the sauce and sausage mixture.
6. Place bell pepper chunks in air fryer baking pan and cook for 8 minutes or until tender. When done, stir into sauce

with sausage and other vegetables.

7. Serve over cooked spaghetti with plenty of Parmesan cheese.

Variations & Ingredients Tips:

- Use hot or sweet Italian sausage for more or less spice
- Add sliced zucchini, eggplant or other veggies to the mix
- Finish with a splash of red wine or balsamic vinegar for extra flavor

Per Serving: Calories: 316; Total Fat: 16g; Saturated Fat: 5g; Cholesterol: 41mg; Sodium: 920mg; Total Carbs: 27g; Dietary Fiber: 4g; Total Sugars: 9g; Protein: 17g

Easy-peasy Beef Sliders

Servings: 4 | Prep Time: 10 Minutes | Cooking Time: 25 Minutes

Ingredients:

- 454g ground beef
- 1/4 tsp cumin
- 1/4 tsp mustard powder
- 1/3 cup grated yellow onion
- 1/2 tsp smoked paprika
- Salt and pepper to taste

Directions:

1. Preheat air fryer to 175°C/350°F. Combine the ground beef, cumin, mustard, onion, paprika, salt, and black pepper in a bowl. Form mixture into 8 patties and make a slight indentation in the middle of each. Place beef patties in the greased frying basket and Air Fry for 8-10 minutes, flipping once. Serve right away and enjoy!

Variations & Ingredients Tips:

- Use ground turkey or chicken instead of beef
- Add shredded cheese like cheddar to the patty mixture
- Brush patties with BBQ sauce or garlic butter before serving

Per Serving: Calories: 265; Total Fat: 16g; Saturated Fat: 6g; Cholesterol: 75mg; Sodium: 185mg; Total Carbs: 2g; Dietary Fiber: 1g; Total Sugars: 1g; Protein: 26g

Rosemary T-bone

Servings: 2 | Prep Time: 10 Minutes | Cooking Time: 20 Minutes

Ingredients:

- 2 tablespoons butter, softened
- ¼ teaspoon lemon juice
- 2 cloves garlic, minced
- 1 teaspoon minced fresh rosemary
- 1 beef T-bone steak
- Salt and pepper to taste
- ¼ teaspoon onion powder

Directions:

1. In a small bowl, whisk butter, lemon juice, onion powder, garlic, and rosemary. Transfer the butter mixture onto parchment paper. Roll into a log and spin ends to tighten. Let chill in the fridge for 2 hours. Remove the steak from the fridge 30 minutes before cooking. Season.
2. Preheat air fryer to 200°C/400°F. Add the steak to the greased frying basket and Air Fry for 10 minutes, flipping once. Transfer steak to a cutting board and let sit for 5 minutes. Cut butter mixture into slices and top the steak. Let the butter melts over before serving. Enjoy!

Variations & Ingredients Tips:

- Try different herb butters like thyme, sage or basil
- Add some blue cheese crumbles to the butter for a tangy twist
- Serve with roasted garlic mashed potatoes or grilled asparagus

Per Serving: Calories: 580; Total Fat: 46g; Saturated Fat: 23g; Cholesterol: 168mg; Sodium: 233mg; Total Carbs: 1g; Dietary Fiber: 0g; Total Sugars: 0g; Protein: 41g

Citrus Pork Lettuce Wraps

Servings: 4 | Prep Time: 15 Minutes | Cooking Time: 35 Minutes

Ingredients:

- Salt and white pepper to taste
- 1 tablespoon cornstarch
- 1 tablespoon red wine vinegar
- 2 tablespoons orange marmalade
- 1 teaspoon pulp-free orange juice
- 2 teaspoons olive oil
- ¼ teaspoon chili pepper
- ¼ teaspoon ground ginger
- 450 g pork loin, cubed
- 8 iceberg lettuce leaves

Directions:

1. Create a slurry by whisking cornstarch and 1 tablespoon of water in a bowl. Set aside. Place a small saucepan over medium heat. Add the red wine vinegar, orange marmalade, orange juice, olive oil, chili pepper, and ginger and cook for 3 minutes, stirring continuously. Mix in the slurry and simmer for 1 more minute. Turn the heat off and let it thicken, about 3 minutes.
2. Preheat air fryer to 180°C/350°F. Sprinkle the pork with salt and white pepper. Place them in the greased frying basket and Air Fry for 8-10 minutes until cooked through and browned, turning once. Transfer pork cubes to a bowl with the sauce and toss to coat. Serve in lettuce leaves.

Variations & Ingredients Tips:

- Use different types of citrus, such as lemon or lime, for a variety of flavors.

- Add some minced garlic or shallots to the sauce for extra flavor.
- Serve the pork lettuce wraps with a side of rice or noodles for a complete meal.

Per Serving: Calories: 260; Total Fat: 9g; Saturated Fat: 2g; Cholesterol: 75mg; Sodium: 140mg; Total Carbs: 19g; Fiber: 1g; Sugars: 14g; Protein: 27g

Mushroom & Quinoa-stuffed Pork Loins

Servings: 3 | Prep Time: 20 Minutes | Cooking Time: 25 Minutes

Ingredients:

- 3 boneless center-cut pork loins, pocket cut in each loin
- ½ cup diced white mushrooms
- 1 teaspoon vegetable oil
- 3 bacon slices, diced
- ½ onion, peeled and diced
- 1 cup baby spinach
- Salt and pepper to taste
- ½ cup cooked quinoa
- ½ cup mozzarella cheese

Directions:

1. Warm the oil in a skillet over medium heat. Add the bacon and cook for 3 minutes until the fat is rendered but not crispy. Add in onion and mushrooms and stir-fry for 3 minutes until the onions are translucent. Stir in spinach, salt, and pepper and cook for 1 minute until the spinach wilts. Set aside and toss in quinoa.
2. Preheat air fryer at 180°C/350°F. Stuff quinoa mixture into each pork loin and sprinkle with mozzarella cheese. Place them in the frying basket and Air Fry for 11 minutes.
3. Let rest onto a cutting board for 5 minutes before serving.

Variations & Ingredients Tips:

- Use different types of mushrooms, such as shiitake or portobello, for a variety of flavors and textures.
- Add some chopped nuts, such as walnuts or pecans, to the quinoa mixture for a crunchy texture.
- Serve the stuffed pork loins with a side of roasted vegetables or a salad for a complete meal.

Per Serving: Calories: 430; Total Fat: 24g; Saturated Fat: 9g; Cholesterol: 115mg; Sodium: 470mg; Total Carbs: 8g; Fiber: 1g; Sugars: 1g; Protein: 45g

Kawaii Pork Roast

Servings: 6 | Prep Time: 10 Minutes | Cooking Time: 50 Minutes

Ingredients:

- Salt and white pepper to taste
- 2 tbsp soy sauce
- 2 tbsp honey
- 1 tbsp sesame oil
- 1/4 tsp ground ginger
- 1 tsp oregano
- 2 cloves garlic, minced
- 1 boneless pork loin (around 1.4kg)

Directions:

1. Preheat air fryer at 350°F/177°C. Mix all ingredients in a bowl. Massage mixture into all sides of pork loin. Place pork loin in the greased frying basket and Roast for 40 minutes, flipping once. Let rest onto a cutting board for 5 minutes before slicing into 25cm thick slices. Serve right away.

Variations & Ingredients Tips:

- Add grated ginger or Chinese five-spice powder for more flavor
- Brush the roast with additional honey glaze halfway through cooking
- Serve sliced pork over rice or sliced on sandwiches

Per Serving: Calories: 300; Total Fat: 14g; Saturated Fat: 4g; Cholesterol: 100mg; Sodium: 500mg; Total Carbs: 8g; Dietary Fiber: 0g; Total Sugars: 6g; Protein: 35g

Beef Fajitas

Servings: 2 | Prep Time: 5 Minutes | Cooking Time: 15 Minutes

Ingredients:

- 225 g sliced mushrooms
- ½ onion, cut into half-moons
- 1 tbsp olive oil
- Salt and pepper to taste
- 1 strip steak
- ½ tsp smoked paprika
- ½ tsp fajita seasoning
- 2 tbsp corn

Directions:

1. Preheat air fryer to 200°C/400°F. Combine the olive oil, onion, and salt in a bowl. Add the mushrooms and toss to coat. Spread in the frying basket. Sprinkle steak with salt, paprika, fajita seasoning and black pepper. Place steak on top of the mushroom mixture and air fry for 9 minutes, flipping steak once. Let rest onto a cutting board for 5 minutes before cutting in half. Divide steak, mushrooms, corn, and onions between 2 plates and serve.

Variations & Ingredients Tips:

- Add sliced bell peppers, jalapeños, or zucchini to the vegetable mixture for extra color and crunch.
- Use chicken, shrimp, or tofu instead of steak for different protein options.
- Serve with warm tortillas, rice, or beans for a complete fajita meal.

Per Serving: Calories: 331; Total Fat: 20g; Saturated Fat: 6g; Cholesterol: 74mg; Sodium: 172mg; Total Carbohydrates: 12g; Dietary Fiber: 2g; Total Sugars: 4g; Protein: 28g

Steakhouse Burgers With Red Onion Compote

Servings: 4 | Prep Time: 25 Minutes | Cooking Time: 22 Minutes

Ingredients:

- 680 g lean ground beef
- 2 cloves garlic, minced and divided
- 1 teaspoon Worcestershire sauce
- 1 teaspoon sea salt, divided
- ½ teaspoon black pepper
- 1 tablespoon extra-virgin olive oil
- 1 red onion, thinly sliced
- 59 g balsamic vinegar
- 1 teaspoon sugar
- 1 tablespoon tomato paste
- 2 tablespoons mayonnaise
- 2 tablespoons sour cream
- 4 brioche hamburger buns
- 1 cup arugula

Directions:

1. In a large bowl, mix together the ground beef, 1 of the minced garlic cloves, the Worcestershire sauce, ½ teaspoon of the salt, and the black pepper. Form the meat into 2.5 cm-thick patties. Make a dent in the center (this helps the center cook evenly). Let the meat sit for 15 minutes.
2. Meanwhile, in a small saucepan over medium heat, cook the olive oil and red onion for 4 minutes, stirring frequently to avoid burning. Add in the balsamic vinegar, sugar, and tomato paste, and cook for an additional 3 minutes, stirring frequently. Transfer the onion compote to a small bowl.
3. Preheat the air fryer to 175°C/350°F.
4. In another small bowl, mix together the remaining minced garlic, the mayonnaise, and the sour cream. Spread the mayo mixture on the insides of the brioche buns.
5. Cook the hamburgers for 6 minutes, flip the burgers, and cook an additional 2 to 6 minutes. Check the internal temperature to avoid under- or overcooking. Hamburgers should be cooked to at least 71°C/160°F. After cooking, cover with foil and let the meat rest for 5 minutes.
6. Meanwhile, place the buns inside the air fryer and toast them for 3 minutes.
7. To assemble the burgers, place the hamburger on one side of the bun, top with onion compote and 59 g arugula, and then place the other half of the bun on top.

Variations & Ingredients Tips:

- Mix some crumbled blue cheese or crispy bacon into the burger patties
- Top with sliced avocado, fried egg or sautéed mushrooms
- Swap arugula for watercress, baby spinach or butter lettuce

Per Serving: Calories: 588; Total Fat: 35g; Saturated Fat: 11g; Cholesterol: 124mg; Sodium: 945mg; Total Carbs: 32g; Dietary Fiber: 2g; Total Sugars: 10g; Protein: 39g

Fusion Tender Flank Steak

Servings: 4 | Prep Time: 15 Minutes | Cooking Time: 25 Minutes

Ingredients:

- 2 tbsp cilantro, chopped
- 2 tbsp chives, chopped
- ¼ tsp red pepper flakes
- 1 jalapeño pepper, minced
- 1 lime, juiced
- 3 tbsp olive oil
- Salt and pepper to taste
- 2 tbsp sesame oil
- 5 tbsp tamari sauce
- 3 tsp honey
- 1 tbsp grated fresh ginger
- 2 green onions, minced
- 2 garlic cloves, minced
- 567 g flank steak

Directions:

1. Combine the jalapeño pepper, cilantro, chives, lime juice, olive oil, salt, and pepper in a bowl. Set aside. Mix the sesame oil, tamari sauce, honey, ginger, green onions, garlic, and pepper flakes in another bowl. Stir until the honey is dissolved. Put the steak into the bowl and massage the marinade onto the meat. Marinate for 2 hours in the fridge. Preheat air fryer to 195°C/390°F.
2. Remove the steak from the marinade and place it in the greased frying basket. Air Fry for about 6 minutes, flip, and continue cooking for 6-8 more minutes. Allow to rest for a few minutes, slice thinly against the grain and top with the prepared dressing. Serve and enjoy!

Variations & Ingredients Tips:

- Swap the flank steak for skirt steak or hanger steak
- Add some sesame seeds to the dressing for crunch and nuttiness
- Serve with steamed rice and stir-fried vegetables for an Asian-inspired meal

Per Serving: Calories: 473; Total Fat: 32g; Saturated Fat: 7g; Cholesterol: 68mg; Sodium: 1590mg; Total Carbs: 13g; Dietary Fiber: 1g; Total Sugars: 9g; Protein: 36g

Beef & Spinach Sautée

Servings: 4 | Prep Time: 10 Minutes | Cooking Time: 30 Minutes

Ingredients:

- 2 tomatoes, chopped
- 2 tbsp crumbled goat cheese
- 225 g ground beef
- 1 shallot, chopped
- 2 garlic cloves, minced
- 2 cups baby spinach
- 2 tbsp lemon juice
- 80 ml beef broth

Directions:

1. Preheat air fryer to 190°C/370°F. Crumble the beef in

a baking pan and place it in the air fryer. Air fry for 3-7 minutes, stirring once. Drain the meat and make sure it's browned. Toss in the tomatoes, shallot, and garlic and air fry for an additional 4-8 minutes until soft. Toss in the spinach, lemon juice, and beef broth and cook for 2-4 minutes until the spinach wilts. Top with goat cheese and serve.

Variations & Ingredients Tips:

- Use ground turkey, chicken, or pork instead of beef for a leaner option.
- Add sliced mushrooms, bell peppers, or zucchini for extra veggies.
- Serve over rice, quinoa, or pasta for a heartier meal.

Per Serving: Calories: 215; Total Fat: 13g; Saturated Fat: 6g; Cholesterol: 56mg; Sodium: 253mg; Total Carbohydrates: 6g; Dietary Fiber: 2g; Total Sugars: 3g; Protein: 17g

Mustard-crusted Rib-eye

Servings: 2 | Prep Time: 35 Minutes | Cooking Time: 9 Minutes

Ingredients:

- Two rib-eye steaks (170 g each), about 2.5 cm thick
- 1 teaspoon coarse salt
- ½ teaspoon coarse black pepper
- 2 tablespoons Dijon mustard

Directions:

1. Rub the steaks with the salt and pepper. Then spread the mustard on both sides of the steaks. Cover with foil and let the steaks sit at room temperature for 30 minutes.
2. Preheat the air fryer to 200°C/390°F.
3. Cook the steaks for 9 minutes. Check for an internal temperature of 60°C/140°F and immediately remove the steaks and let them rest for 5 minutes before slicing.

Variations & Ingredients Tips:

- Use different types of mustard, such as whole grain or spicy brown, for a variety of flavors.
- Add some minced garlic or dried herbs, such as thyme or rosemary, to the mustard coating for extra flavor.
- Serve the rib-eye steaks with a side of roasted vegetables or a baked potato for a classic steakhouse meal.

Per Serving: Calories: 390; Total Fat: 27g; Saturated Fat: 11g; Cholesterol: 115mg; Sodium: 1160mg; Total Carbs: 1g; Fiber: 0g; Sugars: 0g; Protein: 34g

Lemon-garlic Strip Steak

Servings: 2 | Prep Time: 35 Minutes | Cooking Time: 15 Minutes

Ingredients:

- 3 cloves garlic, minced
- 1 tablespoon lemon juice
- 1 tablespoon olive oil
- Salt and pepper to taste
- 1 tablespoon chopped parsley
- ½ teaspoon chopped rosemary
- ½ teaspoon chopped sage
- 1 strip steak

Directions:

1. In a small bowl, whisk all ingredients. Brush mixture over strip steak and let marinate covered in the fridge for 30 minutes.
2. Preheat air fryer at 200°C/400°F. Place strip steak in the greased frying basket and Bake for 8 minutes until rare, turning once.
3. Let rest onto a cutting board for 5 minutes before serving.

Variations & Ingredients Tips:

- Use different types of herbs, such as thyme or oregano, for a variety of flavors.
- Add some red pepper flakes or Dijon mustard to the marinade for a spicy kick.
- Serve the steak with a side of roasted potatoes or a green salad for a complete meal.

Per Serving: Calories: 320; Total Fat: 22g; Saturated Fat: 7g; Cholesterol: 75mg; Sodium: 75mg; Total Carbs: 2g; Fiber: 0g; Sugars: 0g; Protein: 28g

Teriyaki Country-style Pork Ribs

Servings: 3 | Prep Time: 10 Minutes | Cooking Time: 30 Minutes

Ingredients:

- 3 tablespoons Regular or low-sodium soy sauce or gluten-free tamari sauce
- 3 tablespoons Honey
- 3/4 teaspoon Ground dried ginger
- 3/4 teaspoon Garlic powder
- 3 227g boneless country-style pork ribs
- Vegetable oil spray

Directions:

1. Preheat the air fryer to 350°F/177°C.
2. Mix the soy or tamari sauce, honey, ground ginger, and garlic powder in another bowl until uniform.
3. Smear about half of this teriyaki sauce over all sides of the country-style ribs. Reserve the remainder of the teriyaki sauce. Generously coat the meat with vegetable oil spray.
4. When the machine is at temperature, place the country-style ribs in the basket with as much air space between them as possible. Air-fry undisturbed for 15 minutes. Turn the country-style ribs (but keep the space between them) and brush them all over with the remaining teriyaki sauce. Continue air-frying undisturbed for 15 minutes, or until an

instant-read meat thermometer inserted into the center of one rib registers at least 145°F/63°C.

5. Use kitchen tongs to transfer the country-style ribs to a wire rack. Cool for 5 minutes before serving.

Variations & Ingredients Tips:

- Use boneless pork loin or tenderloin instead of country-style ribs
- Add crushed red pepper or sriracha to the teriyaki sauce for extra heat
- Sprinkle with sesame seeds or sliced green onions before serving

Per Serving: Calories: 525; Total Fat: 24g; Saturated Fat: 8g; Cholesterol: 155mg; Sodium: 790mg; Total Carbs: 30g; Dietary Fiber: 0g; Total Sugars: 24g; Protein: 44g

Lamb Chops

Servings: 2 | Prep Time: 5 Minutes (plus Marinating Time) | Cooking Time: 20 Minutes

Ingredients:

- 2 teaspoons oil
- ½ teaspoon ground rosemary
- ½ teaspoon lemon juice
- 450 g lamb chops, approximately 2.5 cm thick
- Salt and pepper
- Cooking spray

Directions:

1. Mix the oil, rosemary, and lemon juice together and rub into all sides of the lamb chops. Season to taste with salt and pepper.
2. For best flavor, cover lamb chops and allow them to rest in the fridge for 20 minutes.
3. Spray air fryer basket with nonstick spray and place lamb chops in it.
4. Cook at 180°C/360°F for approximately 20 minutes. This will cook chops to medium. The meat will be juicy but have no remaining pink. Cook for a minute or two longer for well done chops. For rare chops, stop cooking after about 12 minutes and check for doneness.

Variations & Ingredients Tips:

- Use different herbs, such as thyme or oregano, for a variety of flavors.
- Add some minced garlic or Dijon mustard to the marinade for extra flavor.
- Serve the lamb chops with a side of roasted vegetables or mashed potatoes for a complete meal.

Per Serving: Calories: 450; Total Fat: 32g; Saturated Fat: 13g; Cholesterol: 145mg; Sodium: 130mg; Total Carbs: 0g; Fiber: 0g; Sugars: 0g; Protein: 38g

Wasabi-coated Pork Loin Chops

Servings: 3 | Prep Time: 15 Minutes | Cooking Time: 14 Minutes

Ingredients:

- 1½ cups Wasabi peas
- ¼ cup Plain panko breadcrumbs
- 1 Large egg white
- 2 tablespoons Water
- 3 (142g each) boneless center-cut pork loin chops (about 1.25cm thick)

Directions:

1. Preheat the air fryer to 190°C/375°F.
2. In a food processor, grind wasabi peas until finely ground like panko crumbs. Add breadcrumbs and pulse to blend.
3. Whisk egg white and water in one shallow dish. Place wasabi pea mixture in another shallow dish.
4. Dip pork chops in egg mixture, allowing excess to drip off, then coat in wasabi mixture, pressing gently.
5. Air fry chops for 12 minutes, flipping halfway, until crisp, browned and internal temp reaches 63°C/145°F (may need 2 extra minutes at 182°C/360°F).
6. Transfer chops to a wire rack and let cool briefly before serving.

Variations & Ingredients Tips:

- For extra crunch, double dip the pork chops in the egg and coating mixtures
- Add 1-2 tsp wasabi powder to the coating for more heat
- Substitute panko with regular breadcrumbs if desired

Per Serving: Calories: 310; Total Fat: 12g; Saturated Fat: 3g; Cholesterol: 105mg; Sodium: 520mg; Total Carbs: 18g; Dietary Fiber: 2g; Total Sugars: 2g; Protein: 33g

Cheesy Mushroom-stuffed Pork Loins

Servings: 3 | Prep Time: 10 Minutes | Cooking Time: 30 Minutes

Ingredients:

- 3/4 cup diced mushrooms
- 2 tsp olive oil
- 1 shallot, diced
- Salt and pepper to taste
- 3 center-cut pork loins
- 6 Gruyère cheese slices

Directions:

1. Warm the olive oil in a skillet over medium heat. Add in shallot and mushrooms and stir-fry for 3 minutes. Sprinkle with salt and pepper and cook for 1 minute.
2. Preheat air fryer to 177°C/350°F. Cut a pocket into each pork loin and set aside. Stuff an even amount of mushroom mixture into each chop pocket and top with 2 Gruyere

cheese slices into each pocket. Place the pork in the lightly greased frying basket and Air Fry for 11 minutes cooked through and the cheese has melted. Let sit onto a cutting board for 5 minutes before serving.

Variations & Ingredients Tips:

- Use button or baby bella mushrooms instead of regular white mushrooms
- Add garlic, thyme or other fresh herbs to the mushroom stuffing
- Substitute Swiss, provolone or cheddar for the Gruyere cheese

Per Serving: Calories: 350; Total Fat: 20g; Saturated Fat: 8g; Cholesterol: 110mg; Sodium: 320mg; Total Carbohydrates: 4g; Dietary Fiber: 1g; Total Sugars: 1g; Protein: 37g

Seedy Rib Eye Steak Bites

Servings: 4 | Prep Time: 10 Minutes | Cooking Time: 20 Minutes

Ingredients:

- 454 g rib eye steak, cubed
- 2 garlic cloves, minced
- 2 tablespoons olive oil
- 1 tablespoon thyme, chopped
- 1 teaspoon ground fennel seeds
- Salt and pepper to taste
- 1 onion, thinly sliced

Directions:

1. Preheat air fryer to 190°C/380°F. Place the steak, garlic, olive oil, thyme, fennel seeds, salt, pepper, and onion in a bowl. Mix until all of the beef and onion are well coated. Put the seasoned steak mixture into the frying basket. Roast for 10 minutes, stirring once. Let sit for 5 minutes. Serve.

Variations & Ingredients Tips:

- Use sirloin, flank or skirt steak instead of ribeye
- Add some sliced bell peppers or mushrooms to the mix
- Serve over rice, pasta or salad greens for a complete meal

Per Serving: Calories: 318; Total Fat: 23g; Saturated Fat: 8g; Cholesterol: 81mg; Sodium: 100mg; Total Carbs: 3g; Dietary Fiber: 1g; Total Sugars: 1g; Protein: 24g

Zesty London Broil

Servings: 4 | Prep Time: 15 Minutes | Cooking Time: 28 Minutes

Ingredients:

- ⅔ cup ketchup
- ¼ cup honey
- ¼ cup olive oil
- 2 tablespoons apple cider vinegar
- 2 tablespoons Worcestershire sauce
- 2 tablespoons minced onion
- ½ teaspoon paprika
- 1 teaspoon salt
- 1 teaspoon freshly ground black pepper
- 907g London broil, top round or flank steak (about 2.5cm thick)

Directions:

1. Combine the ketchup, honey, olive oil, apple cider vinegar, Worcestershire sauce, minced onion, paprika, salt and pepper in a small bowl and whisk together.
2. Generously pierce both sides of the meat with a fork or meat tenderizer and place it in a shallow dish. Pour the marinade mixture over the steak, making sure all sides get coated. Cover and refrigerate overnight.
3. Preheat the air fryer to 205°C/400°F.
4. Transfer the London broil to the air fryer basket and air fry for 28 minutes, flipping halfway through, until desired doneness is reached.
5. Remove steak and let rest 5 minutes before thinly slicing against the grain. Transfer to a platter to serve.

Variations & Ingredients Tips:

- Use balsamic vinegar instead of apple cider for a deeper flavor
- Add 1-2 tsp spicy brown mustard to the marinade
- Substitute honey with maple syrup or brown sugar

Per Serving: Calories: 465; Total Fat: 23g; Saturated Fat: 6g; Cholesterol: 100mg; Sodium: 820mg; Total Carbs: 23g; Dietary Fiber: 1g; Total Sugars: 18g; Protein: 40g

Exotic Pork Skewers

Servings: 4 | Prep Time: 20 Minutes | Cooking Time: 30 Minutes

Ingredients:

- 1/3 cup apricot jam
- 2 tbsp lemon juice
- 2 tsp olive oil
- ½ tsp dried tarragon
- 454 g pork tenderloin, cubed
- 4 pitted cherries, halved
- 4 pitted apricots, halved

Directions:

1. Preheat air fryer to 190°C/380°F. Toss the jam, lemon juice, olive oil, and tarragon in a big bowl and mix well.
2. Place the pork in the bowl, then stir well to coat. Allow marinating for 10 minutes.
3. Poke 4 metal skewers through the pork, cherries, and apricots, alternating ingredients. Use a cooking brush to rub the marinade on the skewers, then place them in the air fryer. Toss the rest of the marinade.
4. Air Fry the kebabs for 4-6 minutes on each side until the pork is cooked through and the fruit is soft. Serve!

Variations & Ingredients Tips:

- Try using different jams like peach or cherry for a different flavor profile
- Add some red pepper flakes to the marinade for a spicy kick
- Soak the skewers in water for 30 minutes before using to prevent burning

Per Serving: Calories: 306; Total Fat: 8g; Saturated Fat: 2g; Cholesterol: 83mg; Sodium: 71mg; Total Carbs: 29g; Dietary Fiber: 1g; Total Sugars: 25g; Protein: 30g

Sriracha Short Ribs

Servings: 4 | Prep Time: 5 Minutes | Cooking Time: 15 Minutes

Ingredients:

- 10 g sesame seeds
- 8 pork short ribs
- 118 g soy sauce
- 59 g rice wine vinegar
- 118 g chopped onion
- 2 garlic cloves, minced
- 15 g sesame oil
- 5 g sriracha
- 4 scallions, thinly sliced
- Salt and pepper to taste

Directions:

1. Put short ribs in a resealable bag along with soy sauce, vinegar, onion, garlic, sesame oil, Sriracha, half of the scallions, salt, and pepper. Seal the bag and toss to coat. Refrigerate for one hour.
2. Preheat air fryer to 190°C/380°F. Place the short ribs in the air fryer. Bake for 8-10 minutes, flipping once until crisp. When the ribs are done, garnish with remaining scallions and sesame seeds. Serve and enjoy!

Variations & Ingredients Tips:

- Use beef short ribs or country-style pork ribs for meatier bites
- Brush the ribs with honey or brown sugar in the last few minutes of cooking for a sticky glaze
- Serve with kimchi, pickled radish and steamed rice

Per Serving: Calories: 535; Total Fat: 43g; Saturated Fat: 14g; Cholesterol: 113mg; Sodium: 2319mg; Total Carbs: 9g; Dietary Fiber: 1g; Total Sugars: 3g; Protein: 27g

Vegetarian Recipes

Ricotta & Broccoli Cannelloni

Servings: 4 | Prep Time: 15 Minutes | Cooking Time: 35 Minutes

Ingredients:

- 1 cup shredded mozzarella cheese
- 1/2 cup cooked broccoli, chopped
- 1/2 cup cooked spinach, chopped
- 4 cooked cannelloni shells
- 1 cup ricotta cheese
- 1/2 tsp dried marjoram
- 1 egg
- 1 cup passata (tomato sauce)
- 1 tbsp fresh basil leaves

Directions:

1. Preheat air fryer to 182°C/360°F.
2. Beat the egg in a bowl. Add ricotta, marjoram, 1/2 cup mozzarella, broccoli and spinach. Stir to combine.
3. Spread some passata in the base of a baking dish.
4. Fill the cannelloni shells with the ricotta mixture and place over the passata.
5. Top with remaining passata and mozzarella.
6. Place dish in air fryer basket and bake for 25 minutes until cheese is melted and golden.
7. Garnish with fresh basil before serving.

Variations & Ingredients Tips:

- Use a store-bought marinara or arrabiata sauce instead of passata.
- Add cooked chicken or sausage to the ricotta filling.
- Top with grated parmesan along with the mozzarella.

Per Serving: Calories: 366; Total Fat: 20g; Saturated Fat: 11g; Cholesterol: 89mg; Sodium: 584mg; Total Carbs: 30g; Fiber: 4g; Sugars: 7g; Protein: 21g

Chive Potato Pierogi

Servings: 4 | Prep Time: 25 Minutes | Cooking Time: 55 Minutes

Ingredients:

- 2 boiled potatoes (around 340g), mashed
- Salt and pepper to taste
- 1 tsp cumin powder
- 2 tbsp sour cream
- 1/4 cup grated Parmesan
- 2 tbsp chopped chives
- 1 tbsp chopped parsley

- 1 1/4 cups flour
- 1/4 tsp garlic powder
- 3/4 cup Greek yogurt
- 1 egg
- Cooking spray or oil for greasing

Directions:

1. Combine the mashed potatoes along with sour cream, cumin, parsley, chives, pepper, and salt and stir until slightly chunky.
2. Mix the flour, salt, and garlic powder in a large bowl. Stir in yogurt until it comes together as a sticky dough. Knead in the bowl for about 2-3 minutes to make it smooth.
3. Whisk the egg and 1 teaspoon of water in a small bowl.
4. Roll out the dough on a lightly floured work surface to 6-mm thickness. Cut out 12 circles with a cookie cutter.
5. Preheat air fryer to 175°C/350°F.
6. Divide the potato mixture and Parmesan cheese between the dough circles. Brush the edges with the egg wash and fold the dough over the filling into half-moon shapes. Crimp the edges with a fork to seal.
7. Arrange the pierogies on the greased frying basket and Air Fry for 8-10 minutes, turning once, until the outside is golden.
8. Serve warm.

Variations & Ingredients Tips:

- Add cooked bacon or caramelized onions to the potato filling for extra flavor.
- Substitute Greek yogurt with sour cream or milk in the dough if desired.
- Serve with a side of sauteed mushrooms or roasted vegetables.

Per Serving (3 pierogies): Calories: 320, Total Fat: 9g, Saturated Fat: 4g, Cholesterol: 60mg, Sodium: 310mg, Total Carbs: 46g, Dietary Fiber: 3g, Total Sugars: 3g, Protein: 12g

Golden Breaded Mushrooms

Servings: 2 | Prep Time: 15 Minutes | Cooking Time: 20 Minutes

Ingredients:

- 2 cups crispy rice cereal
- 1 tsp nutritional yeast
- 2 tsp garlic powder
- 1 tsp dried oregano
- 1 tsp dried basil
- Salt to taste
- 1 tbsp Dijon mustard
- 1 tbsp mayonnaise
- 1/4 cup milk
- 225g whole mushrooms
- 4 tbsp chili sauce
- 3 tbsp mayonnaise

Directions:

1. Preheat air fryer at 175°C/350°F.
2. Blend rice cereal, garlic powder, oregano, basil, nutritional yeast, and salt in a food processor until it gets a breadcrumb consistency. Set aside in a bowl.
3. Mix the mustard, 1 tbsp mayonnaise, and milk in a bowl. Dip mushrooms in the mustard mixture; shake off excess. Then, dredge them in the breadcrumbs; shake off excess.
4. Place mushrooms in the greased frying basket and Air Fry for 7 minutes, shaking once.
5. Mix the 3 tbsp mayonnaise with chili sauce in a small bowl. Serve the mushrooms with the dipping sauce on the side.

Variations & Ingredients Tips:

- Use panko breadcrumbs instead of rice cereal for extra crunch.
- Add paprika or cayenne to the breading for a kick of spice.
- Stuff the mushroom caps with cheese or pesto before breading.

Per Serving: Calories: 340; Total Fat: 20g; Saturated Fat: 3g; Sodium: 900mg; Total Carbs: 35g; Dietary Fiber: 3g; Total Sugars: 6g; Protein: 7g

Party Giant Nachos

Servings: 2 | Prep Time: 10 Minutes | Cooking Time: 20 Minutes

Ingredients:

- 2 tbsp sour cream
- ½ tsp chili powder
- Salt to taste
- 2 soft corn tortillas
- 2 tsp avocado oil
- ½ cup refried beans
- ¼ cup cheddar cheese shreds
- 2 tbsp Parmesan cheese
- 2 tbsp sliced black olives
- ¼ cup torn iceberg lettuce
- ¼ cup baby spinach
- ½ sliced avocado
- 1 tomato, diced
- 2 lime wedges

Directions:

1. Preheat air fryer at 200°C/400°F.
2. Whisk the sour cream, chili powder, and salt in a small bowl.
3. Brush tortillas with avocado oil and season one side with salt. Place tortillas in the air fryer basket and Bake for 3 minutes. Set aside.
4. Layer the refried beans, Parmesan and cheddar cheeses in the tortillas. Place them back into the basket and Bake for 2 minutes.
5. Divide tortillas into 2 serving plates. Top each tortilla with black olives, baby spinach, lettuce, and tomatoes. Dollop sour cream mixture on each.
6. Serve with lime and avocado wedges on the side.

Variations & Ingredients Tips:

- Add sliced jalapeños or hot sauce for a spicy kick.
- Use Greek yogurt instead of sour cream for a healthier option.
- Substitute refried beans with black beans or pinto beans.

Per Serving: Calories: 380; Total Fat: 24g; Saturated Fat: 7g; Sodium: 780mg; Total Carbohydrates: 32g; Dietary Fiber: 9g;

Total Sugars: 5g; Protein: 13g

Vegan Buddha Bowls

Servings: 2 | Prep Time: 20 Minutes | Cooking Time: 45 Minutes

Ingredients:

- 1/2 cup quinoa
- 1 cup sweet potato cubes
- 340 grams broccoli florets
- 3/4 cup bread crumbs
- 1/4 cup chickpea flour
- 1/4 cup hot sauce
- 454 grams super-firm tofu, cubed
- 1 tsp lemon juice
- 2 tsp olive oil
- Salt to taste
- 2 scallions, thinly sliced
- 1 tbsp sesame seeds

Directions:

1. Preheat air fryer to 200°C/400°F.
2. Add quinoa and 1 cup of boiling water in a baking pan, cover it with aluminum foil, and Air Fry for 10 minutes. Set aside covered.
3. Put the sweet potatoes in the air fryer basket and Air Fry for 2 minutes. Add in broccoli and Air Fry for 5 more minutes. Shake up and cook for another 3 minutes. Set the veggies aside.
4. On a plate, put the breadcrumbs. In a bowl, whisk chickpea flour and hot sauce. Toss in tofu cubes until coated and dip them in the breadcrumbs.
5. Air Fry tofu for 10 minutes until crispy.
6. Share quinoa and fried veggies into 2 bowls. Top with crispy tofu and drizzle with lemon juice, olive oil and salt to taste.
7. Scatter with scallions and sesame seeds before serving.

Variations & Ingredients Tips:

- Use cauliflower, Brussels sprouts, or carrots instead of broccoli.
- Substitute quinoa with brown rice, farro, or couscous.
- Add avocado slices or hummus for extra creaminess.

Per Serving: Calories: 620; Total Fat: 26g; Saturated Fat: 3.5g; Sodium: 1120mg; Total Carbohydrates: 71g; Dietary Fiber: 11g; Total Sugars: 9g; Protein: 35g

Chicano Rice Bowls

Servings: 4 | Prep Time: 15 Minutes | Cooking Time: 10 Minutes

Ingredients:

- 1 cup sour cream
- 2 tbsp milk
- 1 tsp ground cumin
- 1 tsp chili powder
- 1/8 tsp cayenne pepper
- 1 tbsp tomato paste
- 1 white onion, chopped
- 1 clove garlic, minced
- ½ tsp ground turmeric
- ½ tsp salt
- 1 cup canned black beans
- 1 cup canned corn kernels
- 1 tsp olive oil
- 4 cups cooked brown rice
- 3 tomatoes, diced
- 1 avocado, diced

Directions:

1. Whisk the sour cream, milk, cumin, ground turmeric, chili powder, cayenne pepper, and salt in a bowl. Let chill covered in the fridge until ready to use.
2. Preheat air fryer at 175°C/350°F. Combine beans, white onion, tomato paste, garlic, corn, and olive oil in a bowl. Transfer it into the frying basket and Air Fry for 5 minutes. Divide cooked rice into 4 serving bowls. Top each with bean mixture, tomatoes, and avocado and drizzle with sour cream mixture over. Serve immediately.

Variations & Ingredients Tips:

- Use quinoa, barley, or farro instead of brown rice for a different grain.
- Add shredded lettuce, salsa, or pickled jalapeños for extra toppings.
- Substitute sour cream with Greek yogurt or cashew cream for a lighter option.

Per Serving: Calories: 510; Cholesterol: 20mg; Total Fat: 22g; Saturated Fat: 8g; Sodium: 670mg; Total Carbohydrates: 70g; Dietary Fiber: 13g; Total Sugars: 9g; Protein: 15g

Thyme Meatless Patties

Servings: 3 | Prep Time: 10 Minutes | Cooking Time: 25 Minutes

Ingredients:

- ½ cup oat flour
- 1 tsp allspice
- ½ tsp ground thyme
- 1 tsp maple syrup
- ½ tsp liquid smoke
- 1 tsp balsamic vinegar

Directions:

1. Preheat air fryer to 200°C/400°F.
2. Mix the oat flour, allspice, thyme, maple syrup, liquid smoke, balsamic vinegar, and 2 tbsp of water in a bowl.
3. Make 6 patties out of the mixture. Place them onto a parchment paper and flatten them to 1-cm thick. Grease the patties with cooking spray.
4. Grill for 12 minutes until crispy, turning once.
5. Serve warm.

Variations & Ingredients Tips:

- Add finely chopped walnuts, sunflower seeds, or pumpkin seeds for crunch.
- Use date syrup or agave nectar instead of maple syrup.
- Serve with a dipping sauce like BBQ, ketchup, or sweet

chili sauce.

Per Serving: Calories: 110; Total Fat: 2g; Saturated Fat: 0g; Sodium: 5mg; Total Carbohydrates: 19g; Dietary Fiber: 2g; Total Sugars: 4g; Protein: 3g

Egg Rolls

Servings: 4 | Prep Time: 20 Minutes | Cooking Time: 8 Minutes

Ingredients:

- 1 clove garlic, minced
- 1 teaspoon sesame oil
- 1 teaspoon olive oil
- ½ cup chopped celery
- ½ cup grated carrots
- 2 green onions, chopped
- 55 grams mushrooms, chopped
- 2 cups shredded Napa cabbage
- 1 teaspoon low-sodium soy sauce
- 1 teaspoon cornstarch
- salt
- 1 egg
- 1 tablespoon water
- 4 egg roll wraps
- olive oil for misting or cooking spray

Directions:

1. In a large skillet, sauté garlic in sesame and olive oils over medium heat for 1 minute.
2. Add celery, carrots, onions, and mushrooms to skillet. Cook 1 minute, stirring.
3. Stir in cabbage, cover, and cook for 1 minute or just until cabbage slightly wilts.
4. In a small bowl, mix soy sauce and cornstarch. Stir into vegetables to thicken. Remove from heat. Salt to taste if needed.
5. Beat together egg and water in a small bowl.
6. Divide filling into 4 portions and roll up in egg roll wraps. Brush all over with egg wash to seal.
7. Mist egg rolls very lightly with olive oil or cooking spray and place in air fryer basket.
8. Cook at 200°C/390°F for 4 minutes. Turn over and cook 4 more minutes, until golden brown and crispy.

Variations & Ingredients Tips:

- Use ground pork, chicken, or tofu for a protein-packed filling.
- Add bean sprouts, bamboo shoots, or water chestnuts for extra crunch.
- Serve with sweet and sour sauce, hoisin sauce, or hot mustard for dipping.

Per Serving (1 egg roll): Calories: 140; Cholesterol: 50mg; Total Fat: 5g; Saturated Fat: 1g; Sodium: 300mg; Total Carbohydrates: 18g; Dietary Fiber: 2g; Total Sugars: 2g; Protein: 5g

Fried Rice With Curried Tofu

Servings: 4 | Prep Time: 10 Minutes | Cooking Time: 25 Minutes

Ingredients:

- 225g extra-firm tofu, cubed
- 1/2 cup canned coconut milk
- 2 tsp red curry paste
- 2 cloves garlic, minced
- 1 tbsp avocado oil
- 1 tbsp coconut oil
- 2 cups cooked rice
- 1 tbsp turmeric powder
- Salt and pepper to taste
- 4 lime wedges
- 1/4 cup chopped cilantro

Directions:

1. Preheat air fryer to 175°C/350°F.
2. Combine tofu, coconut milk, curry paste, garlic, and avocado oil in a bowl. Pour the mixture into a baking pan. Place the pan in the frying basket and Air Fry for 10 minutes, stirring once.
3. Melt the coconut oil in a skillet over medium heat. Add in rice, turmeric powder, salt, and black pepper, and cook for 2 minutes or until heated through.
4. Divide the cooked rice between 4 medium bowls and top with tofu mixture and sauce. Top with cilantro and lime wedges to serve.

Variations & Ingredients Tips:

- Use brown rice or quinoa for extra fiber and nutrients.
- Add diced bell peppers or carrots for extra veggies.
- Top with cashews or peanuts for a crunchy texture.

Per Serving: Calories: 330; Total Fat: 21g; Saturated Fat: 9g; Sodium: 125mg; Total Carbs: 27g; Dietary Fiber: 3g; Total Sugars: 1g; Protein: 11g

Vegetarian Shepherd's Pie

Servings: 4 | Prep Time: 15 Minutes | Cooking Time: 40 Minutes

Ingredients:

- 1 russet potato, peeled and diced
- 1 tbsp olive oil
- 2 tbsp balsamic vinegar
- 1/4 cup cheddar shreds
- 2 tbsp milk
- Salt and pepper to taste
- 2 tsp avocado oil
- 1 cup beefless grounds
- 1/2 onion, diced
- 3 cloves garlic
- 1 carrot, diced
- 1/4 diced green bell peppers
- 1 celery stalk, diced
- 2/3 cup tomato sauce
- 1 tsp chopped rosemary
- 1 tbsp sesame seeds
- 1 tsp thyme leaves
- 1 lemon

Directions:

1. Add salted water to a pot over high heat and bring it to a boil. Add in diced potatoes and cook for 5 minutes until fork tender. Drain and transfer it to a bowl. Add in the olive oil cheddar shreds, milk, salt, and pepper and mash it until

smooth. Set the potato topping aside.

2. Preheat air fryer at 180°C/350°F. Place avocado oil, beefless grounds, garlic, onion, carrot, bell pepper, and celery in a skillet over medium heat and cook for 4 minutes until the veggies are tender.
3. Stir in the remaining ingredients and turn the heat off. Spoon the filling into a greased cake pan. Top with the potato topping.
4. Using tines of a fork, create shallow lines along the top of mashed potatoes. Place cake pan in the frying basket and Bake for 12 minutes.
5. Let rest for 10 minutes before serving sprinkled with sesame seeds and squeezed lemon.

Variations & Ingredients Tips:

- Use different plant-based meat substitutes like soy crumbles.
- Add peas, corn or other veggies to the filling.
- Top with vegan cheese shreds instead of cheddar.

Per Serving: Calories: 278; Total Fat: 11g; Saturated Fat: 3g; Sodium: 665mg; Total Carbohydrates: 38g; Dietary Fiber: 5g; Total Sugars: 8g; Protein: 9g

Roasted Vegetable Pita Pizza

Servings: 4 | Prep Time: 10 Minutes | Cooking Time: 20 Minutes

Ingredients:

- 1 medium red bell pepper, seeded and cut into quarters
- 1 teaspoon extra-virgin olive oil
- ⅛ teaspoon black pepper
- ⅛ teaspoon salt
- Two 15-cm whole-grain pita breads
- 6 tablespoons pesto sauce
- ¼ small red onion, thinly sliced
- ½ cup shredded part-skim mozzarella cheese

Directions:

1. Preheat the air fryer to 200°C/400°F.
2. In a small bowl, toss the bell peppers with the olive oil, pepper, and salt.
3. Place the bell peppers in the air fryer and cook for 15 minutes, shaking every 5 minutes to prevent burning.
4. Remove the peppers and set aside. Turn the air fryer temperature down to 180°C/350°F.
5. Lay the pita bread on a flat surface. Cover each with half the pesto sauce; then top with even portions of the red bell peppers and onions. Sprinkle cheese over the top. Spray the air fryer basket with olive oil mist.
6. Carefully lift the pita bread into the air fryer basket with a spatula.
7. Cook for 5 to 8 minutes, or until the outer edges begin to brown and the cheese is melted.
8. Serve warm with desired sides.

Variations & Ingredients Tips:

- Use hummus or baba ganoush instead of pesto for a Mediterranean flavor.
- Add sliced mushrooms, zucchini, or eggplant for more veggie toppings.
- Sprinkle with red pepper flakes or dried oregano for extra seasoning.

Per Serving: Calories: 240; Total Fat: 12g; Saturated Fat: 3g; Sodium: 480mg; Total Carbohydrates: 26g; Dietary Fiber: 5g; Total Sugars: 4g; Protein: 10g

Meatless Kimchi Bowls

Servings:4 | Prep Time: 10 Minutes | Cooking Time: 20 Minutes

Ingredients:

- 2 cups canned chickpeas
- 1 carrot, julienned
- 6 scallions, sliced
- 1 zucchini, diced
- 2 tbsp coconut aminos
- 2 tsp sesame oil
- 1 tsp rice vinegar
- 2 tsp granulated sugar
- 1 tbsp gochujang
- ¼ tsp salt
- ½ cup kimchi
- 2 tsp roasted sesame seeds

Directions:

1. Preheat air fryer to 180°C/350°F.
2. Combine all ingredients, except for the kimchi, 2 scallions, and sesame seeds, in a baking pan.
3. Place the pan in the air fryer basket and Air Fry for 6 minutes.
4. Toss in kimchi and cook for 2 more minutes.
5. Divide between 2 bowls and garnish with the remaining scallions and sesame seeds.
6. Serve immediately.

Variations & Ingredients Tips:

- Use tempeh or tofu instead of chickpeas for a different protein source.
- Add sliced mushrooms or eggplant for meatier texture.
- Adjust gochujang amount to make it spicier or milder.

Per Serving: Calories: 210; Total Fat: 6g; Saturated Fat: 1g; Sodium: 690mg; Total Carbohydrates: 31g; Dietary Fiber: 8g; Total Sugars: 8g; Protein: 10g

Tomato & Squash Stuffed Mushrooms

Servings:2 | Prep Time: 10 Minutes | Cooking Time: 15 Minutes

Ingredients:

- 12 whole white button mushrooms

- 3 tsp olive oil
- 2 tbsp diced zucchini
- 1 tsp soy sauce
- ¼ tsp salt
- 2 tbsp tomato paste
- 1 tbsp chopped parsley

Directions:

1. Preheat air fryer to 180°C/350°F.
2. Remove the stems from the mushrooms. Chop the stems finely and set in a bowl. Brush 1 tsp of olive oil around the top ridge of mushroom caps.
3. To the bowl of the stem, add all ingredients, except for parsley, and mix.
4. Divide and press mixture into tops of mushroom caps.
5. Place the mushrooms in the air fryer basket and Air Fry for 5 minutes.
6. Top with parsley. Serve.

Variations & Ingredients Tips:

- Use portobello mushrooms instead of button mushrooms for a larger appetizer.
- Substitute zucchini with eggplant, yellow squash, or bell peppers.
- Add grated Parmesan cheese or bread crumbs to the filling for extra flavor and texture.

Per Serving: Calories: 130; Total Fat: 10g; Saturated Fat: 1.5g; Sodium: 490mg; Total Carbohydrates: 7g; Dietary Fiber: 2g; Total Sugars: 4g; Protein: 4g

Powerful Jackfruit Fritters

Servings:4 | Prep Time: 20 Minutes | Cooking Time: 30 Minutes

Ingredients:

- 1 can jackfruit, chopped
- 1 egg, beaten
- 1 tbsp Dijon mustard
- 1 tbsp mayonnaise
- 1 tbsp prepared horseradish
- 2 tbsp grated yellow onion
- 2 tbsp chopped parsley
- 2 tbsp chopped nori
- 2 tbsp flour
- 1 tbsp Cajun seasoning
- ¼ tsp garlic powder
- ¼ tsp salt
- 2 lemon wedges

Directions:

1. In a bowl, combine jackfruit, egg, mustard, mayonnaise, horseradish, onion, parsley, nori, flour, Cajun seasoning, garlic, and salt. Let chill in the fridge for 15 minutes.
2. Preheat air fryer to 180°C/350°F.
3. Divide the mixture into 12 balls. Place them in the air fryer basket and Air Fry for 10 minutes.
4. Serve with lemon wedges.

Variations & Ingredients Tips:

- Substitute jackfruit with canned artichoke hearts or hearts of palm.
- Use Old Bay seasoning instead of Cajun for a different spice profile.
- Serve with tartar sauce or spicy remoulade.

Per Serving: Calories: 120; Total Fat: 5g; Saturated Fat: 1g; Sodium: 730mg; Total Carbohydrates: 16g; Dietary Fiber: 3g; Total Sugars: 6g; Protein: 4g

Healthy Living Mushroom Enchiladas

Servings: 4 | Prep Time: 20 Minutes | Cooking Time: 40 Minutes

Ingredients:

- 2 cups sliced mushrooms
- ½ onion, thinly sliced
- 2 garlic cloves, minced
- 1 tbsp olive oil
- 280 grams spinach, chopped
- ½ tsp ground cumin
- 1 tbsp dried oregano
- 1 tsp chili powder
- ¼ cup grated feta cheese
- ¼ tsp red pepper flakes
- 1 cup grated mozzarella cheese
- 1 cup sour cream
- 2 tbsp mayonnaise
- Juice of 1 lime
- Salt and pepper to taste
- 8 corn tortillas
- 1 jalapeño pepper, diced
- ¼ cup chopped cilantro

Directions:

1. Preheat air fryer to 200°C/400°F.
2. Combine mushrooms, onion, oregano, garlic, chili powder, olive oil, and salt in a small bowl until well coated. Transfer to the greased air fryer basket. Cook for 5 minutes, then shake the basket. Cook for another 3 to 4 minutes, then transfer to a medium bowl.
3. Wipe out the air fryer basket. Take the garlic cloves from the mushroom mixture and finely mince them. Return half of the garlic to the bowl with the mushrooms. Stir in spinach, cumin, red pepper flakes, and ½ cup of mozzarella.
4. Place the other half of the minced garlic in a small bowl along with sour cream, mayonnaise, feta, the rest of the mozzarella, lime juice, and black pepper.
5. To prepare the enchiladas, spoon 2 tablespoons of mushroom mixture in the center of each tortilla. Roll the tortilla and place it seam-side down in the baking dish. Repeat for the rest of the tortillas.
6. Top with sour cream mixture and garnish with jalapeños. Place the dish in the air fryer basket and bake for 20 minutes until heated through and just brown on top.
7. Top with cilantro. Serve.

Variations & Ingredients Tips:

- Substitute mushrooms with zucchini, eggplant, or bell peppers for different veggie options.
- Use flour tortillas instead of corn tortillas for a softer texture.
- Add black beans, corn, or rice to the filling for extra heartiness.

Per Serving: Calories: 450; Cholesterol: 55mg; Total Fat:

31g; Saturated Fat: 13g; Sodium: 620mg; Total Carbohydrates: 34g; Dietary Fiber: 6g; Total Sugars: 7g; Protein: 16g

Charred Cauliflower Tacos

Servings: 4 | Prep Time: 15 Minutes | Cooking Time: 10 Minutes

Ingredients:

- 1 head cauliflower, washed and cut into florets
- 2 tablespoons avocado oil
- 2 teaspoons taco seasoning
- 1 medium avocado
- ½ teaspoon garlic powder
- ¼ teaspoon black pepper
- ¼ teaspoon salt
- 2 tablespoons chopped red onion
- 2 teaspoons fresh squeezed lime juice
- ¼ cup chopped cilantro
- Eight 15-cm corn tortillas
- ½ cup cooked corn
- ½ cup shredded purple cabbage

Directions:

1. Preheat the air fryer to 200°C/390°F.
2. In a large bowl, toss the cauliflower with the avocado oil and taco seasoning. Set the metal trivet inside the air fryer basket and liberally spray with olive oil.
3. Place the cauliflower onto the trivet and cook for 10 minutes, shaking every 3 minutes to allow for an even char.
4. While the cauliflower is cooking, prepare the avocado sauce. In a medium bowl, mash the avocado; then mix in the garlic powder, pepper, salt, and onion. Stir in the lime juice and cilantro; set aside.
5. Remove the cauliflower from the air fryer basket.
6. Place 1 tablespoon of avocado sauce in the middle of a tortilla, and top with corn, cabbage, and charred cauliflower. Repeat with the remaining tortillas. Serve immediately.

Variations & Ingredients Tips:

- Use broccoli, Brussels sprouts, or carrots instead of cauliflower for different veggie options.
- Add sliced radish, pickled onions, or queso fresco for extra toppings.
- Serve with salsa, hot sauce, or lime wedges on the side.

Per Serving (2 tacos): Calories: 380; Cholesterol: 0mg; Total Fat: 20g; Saturated Fat: 3g; Sodium: 520mg; Total Carbohydrates: 47g; Dietary Fiber: 11g; Total Sugars: 7g; Protein: 8g

Mushroom And Fried Onion Quesadilla

Servings: 2 | Prep Time: 15 Minutes | Cooking Time: 33 Minutes

Ingredients:

- 1 onion, sliced
- 2 tablespoons butter, melted
- 280 grams button mushrooms, sliced
- 2 tablespoons Worcestershire sauce
- salt and freshly ground black pepper
- 4 (20-cm) flour tortillas
- 2 cups grated Fontina cheese
- vegetable or olive oil

Directions:

1. Preheat the air fryer to 200°C/400°F.
2. Toss the onion slices with the melted butter and transfer them to the air fryer basket. Air-fry at 200°C/400°F for 15 minutes, shaking the basket several times during the cooking process.
3. Add the mushrooms and Worcestershire sauce to the onions and stir to combine. Air-fry at 200°C/400°F for an additional 10 minutes. Season with salt and freshly ground black pepper.
4. Lay two of the tortillas on a cutting board. Top each tortilla with ½ cup of the grated cheese, half of the onion and mushroom mixture and then finally another ½ cup of the cheese. Place the remaining tortillas on top of the cheese and press down firmly.
5. Brush the air fryer basket with a little oil. Place a quesadilla in the basket and brush the top with a little oil. Secure the top tortilla to the bottom with three toothpicks and air-fry at 200°C/400°F for 5 minutes.
6. Flip the quesadilla over by inverting it onto a plate and sliding it back into the basket. Remove the toothpicks and brush the other side with oil. Air-fry for an additional 3 minutes.
7. Invert the quesadilla onto a cutting board and cut it into 4 or 6 triangles. Serve immediately.

Variations & Ingredients Tips:

- Use any melty cheese like cheddar, Monterey jack, or pepper jack instead of Fontina.
- Add sautéed bell peppers or zucchini for extra veggie goodness.
- Serve with salsa, guacamole, or sour cream for dipping.

Per Serving: Calories: 680; Total Fat: 42g; Saturated Fat: 22g; Sodium: 1160mg; Total Carbohydrates: 51g; Dietary Fiber: 4g; Total Sugars: 6g; Protein: 26g

Spring Veggie Empanadas

Servings: 4 | Prep Time: 45 Minutes | Cooking Time: 75 Minutes

Ingredients:

- 10 empanada pastry discs
- 1 tbsp olive oil
- 1 shallot, minced
- 1 garlic clove, minced
- ½ cup whole milk
- 1 cup chopped broccoli
- ½ cup chopped cauliflower
- ½ cup diced carrots

- ¼ cup diced celery
- ⅛ tsp ground nutmeg
- 1 tsp cumin powder
- 1 tsp minced ginger
- 1 egg

Directions:

1. Melt the olive oil in a pot over medium heat. Stir in shallot and garlic and cook through for 1 minute. Next, add 1 tablespoon of flour and continue stirring. Whisk in milk, then lower the heat.
2. After that, add broccoli, cauliflower, carrots, celery, cumin powder, pepper, ginger, and nutmeg. Cook for 2 minutes then remove from the heat. Allow to cool for 5 minutes.
3. Preheat air fryer to 180°C/350°F. Lightly flour a flat work surface and turn out the pastry discs. Scoop ¼ of the vegetables in the center of each circle.
4. Whisk the egg and 1 teaspoon of water in a small bowl and brush the entire edge of the circle with the egg wash and fold the dough over the filling into a half-moon shape. Crimp the edge with a fork to seal.
5. Arrange the patties in a single layer in the air fryer basket and bake for 12 minutes. Flip the patties and bake for another 10 to 12 minutes until the outside crust is golden.
6. Serve immediately and enjoy.

Variations & Ingredients Tips:

- Use puff pastry or pie crust dough instead of empanada discs.
- Add diced potatoes or sweet potatoes to the filling.
- Serve with a side of salsa, sour cream, or guacamole for dipping.

Per Serving: Calories: 420; Total Fat: 25g; Saturated Fat: 8g; Sodium: 480mg; Total Carbohydrates: 42g; Dietary Fiber: 5g; Total Sugars: 6g; Protein: 11g

Vegetable Couscous

Servings: 4 | Prep Time: 10 Minutes | Cooking Time: 10 Minutes

Ingredients:

- 113g white mushrooms, sliced
- 1/2 medium green bell pepper, julienned
- 1 cup cubed zucchini
- 1/4 small onion, slivered
- 1 stalk celery, thinly sliced
- 1/4 teaspoon ground coriander
- 1/4 teaspoon ground cumin
- Salt and pepper
- 1 tablespoon olive oil
- 3/4 cup uncooked couscous
- 1 cup vegetable broth or water
- 1/2 teaspoon salt (omit if using salted broth)

Directions:

1. Combine all vegetables in a large bowl. Sprinkle with coriander, cumin, and salt and pepper to taste. Stir well, add olive oil, and stir again to coat vegetables evenly.
2. Place vegetables in the air fryer basket and cook at 200°C/390°F for 5 minutes. Stir and cook for 5 more minutes, until tender.
3. While vegetables are cooking, prepare the couscous: Place broth or water and salt in a large saucepan. Heat to boiling, stir in couscous, cover, and remove from heat.
4. Let couscous sit for 5 minutes, stir in cooked vegetables, and serve hot.

Variations & Ingredients Tips:

- Add chickpeas or lentils for extra protein.
- Use different fresh or dried herbs like parsley, thyme or oregano.
- Toss in some feta or goat cheese for a creamy touch.

Per Serving: Calories: 189; Total Fat: 6g; Saturated Fat: 1g; Sodium: 395mg; Total Carbohydrates: 29g; Dietary Fiber: 4g; Total Sugars: 3g; Protein: 6g

Farfalle With White Sauce

Servings: 4 | Prep Time: 10 Minutes | Cooking Time: 30 Minutes

Ingredients:

- 4 cups cauliflower florets
- 1 medium onion, chopped
- 225g farfalle pasta
- 2 tbsp chives, minced
- 1/2 cup cashew pieces
- 1 tbsp nutritional yeast
- 2 large garlic cloves, peeled
- 2 tbsp fresh lemon juice
- Salt and pepper to taste

Directions:

1. Preheat air fryer to 200°C/390°F. Put the cauliflower in the fryer, spray with oil, and Bake for 8 minutes. Remove the basket, stir, and add the onion. Roast for 10 minutes or until the cauliflower is golden and the onions soft.
2. Cook the farfalle pasta according to the package directions. Set aside.
3. Put the roasted cauliflower and onions along with the cashews, 1 1/2 cups of water, yeast, garlic, lemon, salt, and pepper in a blender. Blend until creamy.
4. Pour a large portion of the sauce on top of the warm pasta and add the minced scallions. Serve.

Variations & Ingredients Tips:

- Add roasted garlic for extra flavor depth.
- Substitute cashews with toasted almonds or pine nuts.
- Toss in sautéed spinach or kale for added nutrients.

Per Serving: Calories: 390; Total Fat: 13g; Saturated Fat: 2g; Sodium: 130mg; Total Carbs: 58g; Dietary Fiber: 6g; Total Sugars: 6g; Protein: 14g

Sandwiches And Burgers Recipes

Black Bean Veggie Burgers

Servings: 3 | Prep Time: 15 Minutes | Cooking Time: 10 Minutes

Ingredients:

- 1 cup Drained and rinsed canned black beans
- ⅓ cup Pecan pieces
- ⅓ cup Rolled oats (not quick-cooking or steel-cut; gluten-free, if a concern)
- 2 tablespoons (or 1 small egg) Pasteurized egg substitute, such as Egg Beaters (gluten-free, if a concern)
- 2 teaspoons Red ketchup-like chili sauce, such as Heinz
- ¼ teaspoon Ground cumin
- ¼ teaspoon Dried oregano
- ¼ teaspoon Table salt
- ¼ teaspoon Ground black pepper
- Olive oil
- Olive oil spray

Directions:

1. Preheat the air fryer to 200°C/400°F.
2. Put the beans, pecans, oats, egg substitute or egg, chili sauce, cumin, oregano, salt, and pepper in a food processor. Cover and process to a coarse paste that will hold its shape like sugar-cookie dough, adding olive oil in 1-teaspoon increments to get the mixture to blend smoothly. The amount of olive oil is actually dependent on the internal moisture content of the beans and the oats. Figure on about 1 tablespoon (three 1-teaspoon additions) for the smaller batch, with proportional increases for the other batches. A little too much olive oil can't hurt, but a dry paste will fall apart as it cooks and a far-too-wet paste will stick to the basket.
3. Scrape down and remove the blade. Using clean, wet hands, form the paste into two 10 cm patties for the small batch, three 10 cm patties for the medium, or four 10 cm patties for the large batch, setting them one by one on a cutting board. Generously coat both sides of the patties with olive oil spray.
4. Set them in the basket in one layer. Air-fry undisturbed for 10 minutes, or until lightly browned and crisp at the edges.
5. Use a nonstick-safe spatula, and perhaps a flatware fork for balance, to transfer the burgers to a wire rack. Cool for 5 minutes before serving.

Variations & Ingredients Tips:

- Add finely chopped vegetables like bell peppers, onions, or carrots for extra flavor and nutrition.
- Experiment with different spices and herbs, such as smoked paprika, garlic powder, or cilantro.
- For a gluten-free version, ensure all ingredients are certified gluten-free.

Per Serving: Calories: 280; Cholesterol: 0mg; Total Fat: 15g; Saturated Fat: 2g; Sodium: 420mg; Total Carbohydrates: 28g; Dietary Fiber: 8g; Total Sugars: 2g; Protein: 10g

Inside-out Cheeseburgers

Servings: 3 | Prep Time: 15 Minutes | Cooking Time: 9-11 Minutes

Ingredients:

- 510 grams 90% lean ground beef
- ¾ teaspoon Dried oregano
- ¾ teaspoon Table salt
- ¾ teaspoon Ground black pepper
- ¼ teaspoon Garlic powder
- 6 tablespoons (about 45 grams) Shredded Cheddar, Swiss, or other semi-firm cheese, or a purchased blend of shredded cheeses
- 3 Hamburger buns (gluten-free, if a concern), split open

Directions:

1. Preheat the air fryer to 190°C/375°F.
2. Gently mix the ground beef, oregano, salt, pepper, and garlic powder in a bowl until well combined without turning the mixture to mush. Form it into two 15-cm patties for the small batch, three for the medium, or four for the large.
3. Place 2 tablespoons of the shredded cheese in the center of each patty. With clean hands, fold the sides of the patty up to cover the cheese, then pick it up and roll it gently into a ball to seal the cheese inside. Gently press it back into a 12.5-cm burger without letting any cheese squish out. Continue filling and preparing more burgers, as needed.
4. Place the burgers in the basket in one layer and air-fry undisturbed for 8 minutes for medium or 10 minutes for well-done. (An instant-read meat thermometer won't work for these burgers because it will hit the mostly melted cheese inside and offer a hotter temperature than the surrounding meat.)
5. Use a nonstick-safe spatula, and perhaps a flatware fork for balance, to transfer the burgers to a cutting board. Set the buns cut side down in the basket in one layer (working in batches as necessary) and air-fry undisturbed for 1 minute, to toast a bit and warm up. Cool the burgers a few minutes more, then serve them warm in the buns.

Variations & Ingredients Tips:

- Mix different types of cheese like cheddar, mozzarella, and blue cheese for a flavorful combination.

- Add finely chopped bacon or caramelized onions to the cheese stuffing for extra richness.
- Serve with your favorite burger toppings like lettuce, tomato, onion, and pickles.

Per Serving (1 burger): Calories: 480; Cholesterol: 125mg; Total Fat: 27g; Saturated Fat: 11g; Sodium: 720mg; Total Carbohydrates: 22g; Dietary Fiber: 1g; Total Sugars: 3g; Protein: 38g

Mexican Cheeseburgers

Servings: 4 | Prep Time: 20 Minutes | Cooking Time: 22 Minutes

Ingredients:

- 570 grams ground beef
- ¼ cup finely chopped onion
- ½ cup crushed yellow corn tortilla chips
- 1 (35-gram) packet taco seasoning
- ¼ cup canned diced green chilies
- 1 egg, lightly beaten
- 115 grams pepper jack cheese, grated
- 4 (30-cm) flour tortillas
- shredded lettuce, sour cream, guacamole, salsa (for topping)

Directions:

1. Combine the ground beef, minced onion, crushed tortilla chips, taco seasoning, green chilies, and egg in a large bowl. Mix thoroughly until combined – your hands are good tools for this. Divide the meat into four equal portions and shape each portion into an oval-shaped burger.
2. Preheat the air fryer to 190°C/370°F.
3. Air-fry the burgers for 18 minutes, turning them over halfway through the cooking time. Divide the cheese between the burgers, lower fryer to 170°C/340°F and air-fry for an additional 4 minutes to melt the cheese. (This will give you a burger that is medium-well. If you prefer your cheeseburger medium-rare, shorten the cooking time to about 15 minutes and then add the cheese and proceed with the recipe.)
4. While the burgers are cooking, warm the tortillas wrapped in aluminum foil in a 175°C/350°F oven, or in a skillet with a little oil over medium-high heat for a couple of minutes. Keep the tortillas warm until the burgers are ready.
5. To assemble the burgers, spread sour cream over three quarters of the tortillas and top each with some shredded lettuce and salsa. Place the Mexican cheeseburgers on the lettuce and top with guacamole. Fold the tortillas around the burger, starting with the bottom and then folding the sides in over the top. (A little sour cream can help hold the seam of the tortilla together.) Serve immediately.

Variations & Ingredients Tips:

- Use ground turkey or chicken for a leaner burger option.
- Substitute pepper jack cheese with Monterey Jack or cheddar cheese if preferred.
- Add sliced jalapeños or hot sauce to the burger mixture for extra heat.

Per Serving (1 burger): Calories: 780; Cholesterol: 165mg; Total Fat: 44g; Saturated Fat: 18g; Sodium: 1480mg; Total Carbohydrates: 51g; Dietary Fiber: 4g; Total Sugars: 4g; Protein: 46g

Salmon Burgers

Servings: 3 | Prep Time: 15 Minutes | Cooking Time: 8 Minutes

Ingredients:

- 510 grams Skinless salmon fillet, preferably fattier Atlantic salmon
- 1½ tablespoons Minced chives or the green part of a scallion
- ½ cup Plain panko bread crumbs (gluten-free, if a concern)
- 1½ teaspoons Dijon mustard (gluten-free, if a concern)
- 1½ teaspoons Drained and rinsed capers, minced
- 1½ teaspoons Lemon juice
- ¼ teaspoon Table salt
- ¼ teaspoon Ground black pepper
- Vegetable oil spray

Directions:

1. Preheat the air fryer to 190°C/375°F.
2. Cut the salmon into pieces that will fit in a food processor. Cover and pulse until coarsely chopped. Add the chives and pulse to combine, until the fish is ground but not a paste. Scrape down and remove the blade. Scrape the salmon mixture into a bowl. Add the bread crumbs, mustard, capers, lemon juice, salt, and pepper. Stir gently until well combined.
3. Use clean and dry hands to form the mixture into two 12.5-cm patties for a small batch, three 12.5-cm patties for a medium batch, or four 12.5-cm patties for a large one.
4. Coat both sides of each patty with vegetable oil spray. Set them in the basket in one layer and air-fry undisturbed for 8 minutes, or until browned and an instant-read meat thermometer inserted into the center of a burger registers 65°C/145°F.
5. Use a nonstick-safe spatula, and perhaps a flatware fork for balance, to transfer the burgers to a wire rack. Cool for 2 or 3 minutes before serving.

Variations & Ingredients Tips:

- Substitute salmon with canned or leftover cooked salmon for convenience.
- Add finely chopped red bell pepper or celery to the burger mixture for extra crunch and flavor.
- Serve on toasted buns with lettuce, tomato, and a dollop of tartar sauce or remoulade.

Per Serving (1 burger): Calories: 320; Cholesterol: 95mg; Total Fat: 16g; Saturated Fat: 3g; Sodium: 440mg; Total Carbohydrates: 15g; Dietary Fiber: 1g; Total Sugars: 1g; Protein: 31g

Lamb Burgers

Servings: 3 | Prep Time: 15 Minutes | Cooking Time: 17 Minutes

Ingredients:

- 510 grams Ground lamb
- 3 tablespoons Crumbled feta
- 1 teaspoon Minced garlic
- 1 teaspoon Tomato paste
- ¾ teaspoon Ground coriander
- ¾ teaspoon Ground dried ginger
- Up to ⅛ teaspoon Cayenne
- Up to a ⅛ teaspoon Table salt (optional)
- 3 Kaiser rolls or hamburger buns (gluten-free, if a concern), split open

Directions:

1. Preheat the air fryer to 190°C/375°F.
2. Gently mix the ground lamb, feta, garlic, tomato paste, coriander, ginger, cayenne, and salt (if using) in a bowl until well combined, trying to keep the bits of cheese intact. Form this mixture into two 15-cm patties for the small batch, three 12.5-cm patties for the medium, or four 12.5-cm patties for the large.
3. Set the patties in the basket in one layer and air-fry undisturbed for 16 minutes, or until an instant-read meat thermometer inserted into one burger registers 70°C/160°F. (The cheese is not an issue with the temperature probe in this recipe as it was for the Inside-Out Cheeseburgers, because the feta is so well mixed into the ground meat.)
4. Use a nonstick-safe spatula, and perhaps a flatware fork for balance, to transfer the burgers to a cutting board. Set the buns cut side down in the basket in one layer (working in batches as necessary) and air-fry undisturbed for 1 minute, to toast a bit and warm up. Serve the burgers warm in the buns.

Variations & Ingredients Tips:

- Substitute feta with goat cheese or crumbled blue cheese for a different flavor profile.
- Add finely chopped mint or parsley to the lamb mixture for a fresh, herbal taste.
- Serve with tzatziki sauce, sliced cucumbers, and red onions for a Greek-inspired burger.

Per Serving (1 burger): Calories: 560; Cholesterol: 140mg; Total Fat: 34g; Saturated Fat: 15g; Sodium: 580mg; Total Carbohydrates: 25g; Dietary Fiber: 1g; Total Sugars: 3g; Protein: 38g

Inside Out Cheeseburgers

Servings: 2 | Prep Time: 15 Minutes | Cooking Time: 20 Minutes

Ingredients:

- 340 grams lean ground beef
- 3 tablespoons minced onion
- 4 teaspoons ketchup
- 2 teaspoons yellow mustard
- salt and freshly ground black pepper
- 4 slices of Cheddar cheese, broken into smaller pieces
- 8 hamburger dill pickle chips

Directions:

1. Combine the ground beef, minced onion, ketchup, mustard, salt and pepper in a large bowl. Mix well to thoroughly combine the ingredients. Divide the meat into four equal portions.
2. To make the stuffed burgers, flatten each portion of meat into a thin patty. Place 4 pickle chips and half of the cheese onto the center of two of the patties, leaving a rim around the edge of the patty exposed. Place the remaining two patties on top of the first and press the meat together firmly, sealing the edges tightly. With the burgers on a flat surface, press the sides of the burger with the palm of your hand to create a straight edge. This will help keep the stuffing inside the burger while it cooks.
3. Preheat the air fryer to 190°C/370°F.
4. Place the burgers inside the air fryer basket and air-fry for 20 minutes, flipping the burgers over halfway through the cooking time.
5. Serve the cheeseburgers on buns with lettuce and tomato.

Variations & Ingredients Tips:

- Use different types of cheese like Swiss, pepper jack, or blue cheese for a unique flavor.
- Add crispy bacon pieces or sautéed mushrooms to the stuffing for extra richness.
- Brush the burgers with a mixture of melted butter and minced garlic before cooking for added flavor.

Per Serving (1 burger): Calories: 510; Cholesterol: 145mg; Total Fat: 32g; Saturated Fat: 14g; Sodium: 780mg; Total Carbohydrates: 12g; Dietary Fiber: 1g; Total Sugars: 6g; Protein: 42g

White Bean Veggie Burgers

Servings: 3 | Prep Time: 15 Minutes | Cooking Time: 13 Minutes

Ingredients:

- 320 grams Drained and rinsed canned white beans
- 3 tablespoons Rolled

oats (not quick-cooking or steel-cut; gluten-free, if a concern)
- 3 tablespoons Chopped walnuts
- 2 teaspoons Olive oil
- 2 teaspoons Lemon juice
- 1½ teaspoons Dijon mustard (gluten-free, if a concern)
- ¾ teaspoon Dried sage leaves
- ¼ teaspoon Table salt
- Olive oil spray
- 3 Whole-wheat buns or gluten-free whole-grain buns (if a concern), split open

Directions:

1. Preheat the air fryer to 200°C/400°F.
2. Place the beans, oats, walnuts, oil, lemon juice, mustard, sage, and salt in a food processor. Cover and process to make a coarse paste that will hold its shape, about like wet sugar-cookie dough, stopping the machine to scrape down the inside of the canister at least once.
3. Scrape down and remove the blade. With clean and wet hands, form the bean paste into two 10-cm patties for the small batch, three 10-cm patties for the medium, or four 10-cm patties for the large batch. Generously coat the patties on both sides with olive oil spray.
4. Set them in the basket with some space between them and air-fry undisturbed for 12 minutes, or until lightly brown and crisp at the edges. The tops of the burgers will feel firm to the touch.
5. Use a nonstick-safe spatula, and perhaps a flatware fork for balance, to transfer the burgers to a cutting board. Set the buns cut side down in the basket in one layer (working in batches as necessary) and air-fry undisturbed for 1 minute, to toast a bit and warm up. Serve the burgers warm in the buns.

Variations & Ingredients Tips:

- Use black beans, chickpeas, or lentils instead of white beans for a different flavor and color.
- Add grated carrots, zucchini, or beets to the burger mixture for extra nutrition and texture.
- Serve with your favorite burger toppings like lettuce, tomato, onion, and pickles.

Per Serving (1 burger): Calories: 350; Cholesterol: 0mg; Total Fat: 13g; Saturated Fat: 1g; Sodium: 520mg; Total Carbohydrates: 48g; Dietary Fiber: 9g; Total Sugars: 4g; Protein: 14g

Thanksgiving Turkey Sandwiches

Servings: 3 | Prep Time: 15 Minutes | Cooking Time: 10 Minutes

Ingredients:

- 1½ cups Herb-seasoned stuffing mix (not cornbread-style; gluten-free, if a concern)
- 1 Large egg white(s)
- 2 tablespoons Water
- 3 140- to 170-gram turkey breast cutlets
- Vegetable oil spray
- 4½ tablespoons Purchased cranberry sauce, preferably whole berry
- ⅛ teaspoon Ground cinnamon
- ⅛ teaspoon Ground dried ginger
- 4½ tablespoons Regular, low-fat, or fat-free mayonnaise (gluten-free, if a concern)
- 6 tablespoons Shredded Brussels sprouts
- 3 Kaiser rolls (gluten-free, if a concern), split open

Directions:

1. Preheat the air fryer to 190°C/375°F.
2. Put the stuffing mix in a heavy zip-closed bag, seal it, lay it flat on your counter, and roll a rolling pin over the bag to crush the stuffing mix to the consistency of rough sand. (Or you can pulse the stuffing mix to the desired consistency in a food processor.)
3. Set up and fill two shallow soup plates or small pie plates on your counter: one for the egg white(s), whisked with the water until foamy; and one for the ground stuffing mix.
4. Dip a cutlet in the egg white mixture, coating both sides and letting any excess egg white slip back into the rest. Set the cutlet in the ground stuffing mix and coat it evenly on both sides, pressing gently to coat well on both sides. Lightly coat the cutlet on both sides with vegetable oil spray, set it aside, and continue dipping and coating the remaining cutlets in the same way.
5. Set the cutlets in the basket and air-fry undisturbed for 10 minutes, or until crisp and brown. Use kitchen tongs to transfer the cutlets to a wire rack to cool for a few minutes.
6. Meanwhile, stir the cranberry sauce with the cinnamon and ginger in a small bowl. Mix the shredded Brussels sprouts and mayonnaise in a second bowl until the vegetable is evenly coated.
7. Build the sandwiches by spreading about 1½ tablespoons of the cranberry mixture on the cut side of the bottom half of each roll. Set a cutlet on top, then spread about 3 tablespoons of the Brussels sprouts mixture evenly over the cutlet. Set the other half of the roll on top and serve warm.

Variations & Ingredients Tips:

- Use leftover roasted turkey instead of turkey cutlets for a post-Thanksgiving sandwich.
- Substitute Brussels sprouts with shredded cabbage or kale for a different texture and flavor.
- Add a slice of brie or provolone cheese to the sandwich for extra creaminess.

Per Serving: Calories: 530; Cholesterol: 75mg; Total Fat: 22g; Saturated Fat: 4g; Sodium: 1180mg; Total Carbohydrates: 53g; Dietary Fiber: 4g; Total Sugars: 15g; Protein: 33g

Perfect Burgers

Servings: 3 | Prep Time: 10 Minutes | Cooking Time: 13 Minutes

Ingredients:

- 510 grams 90% lean ground beef
- 1½ tablespoons Worcestershire sauce (gluten-free, if a concern)
- ½ teaspoon Ground black pepper
- 3 Hamburger buns (gluten-free if a concern), split open

Directions:

1. Preheat the air fryer to 190°C/375°F.
2. Gently mix the ground beef, Worcestershire sauce, and pepper in a bowl until well combined but preserving as much of the meat's fibers as possible. Divide this mixture into two 15-cm patties for the small batch, three 12.5-cm patties for the medium, or four 12.5-cm patties for the large. Make a thumbprint indentation in the center of each patty, about halfway through the meat.
3. Set the patties in the basket in one layer with some space between them. Air-fry undisturbed for 10 minutes, or until an instant-read meat thermometer inserted into the center of a burger registers 70°C/160°F (a medium-well burger). You may need to add 2 minutes cooking time if the air fryer is at 180°C/360°F.
4. Use a nonstick-safe spatula, and perhaps a flatware fork for balance, to transfer the burgers to a cutting board. Set the buns cut side down in the basket in one layer (working in batches as necessary) and air-fry undisturbed for 1 minute, to toast a bit and warm up. Serve the burgers in the warm buns.

Variations & Ingredients Tips:

- Mix in finely chopped onions, garlic, or herbs to the burger mixture for extra flavor.
- Use a mixture of ground beef and ground pork or lamb for a juicier, more flavorful burger.
- Top burgers with your favorite cheese, bacon, avocado, or sautéed mushrooms.

Per Serving (1 burger): Calories: 420; Cholesterol: 105mg; Total Fat: 22g; Saturated Fat: 8g; Sodium: 460mg; Total Carbohydrates: 23g; Dietary Fiber: 1g; Total Sugars: 3g; Protein: 34g

Dijon Thyme Burgers

Servings: 3 | Prep Time: 15 Minutes | Cooking Time: 18 Minutes

Ingredients:

- 450 grams lean ground beef
- ⅓ cup panko breadcrumbs
- ¼ cup finely chopped onion
- 3 tablespoons Dijon mustard
- 1 tablespoon chopped fresh thyme
- 4 teaspoons Worcestershire sauce
- 1 teaspoon salt
- freshly ground black pepper
- Topping (optional):
- 2 tablespoons Dijon mustard
- 1 tablespoon dark brown sugar
- 1 teaspoon Worcestershire sauce
- 115 grams sliced Swiss cheese, optional

Directions:

1. Combine all the burger ingredients together in a large bowl and mix well. Divide the meat into 4 equal portions and then form the burgers, being careful not to over-handle the meat. One good way to do this is to throw the meat back and forth from one hand to another, packing the meat each time you catch it. Flatten the balls into patties, making an indentation in the center of each patty with your thumb (this will help it stay flat as it cooks) and flattening the sides of the burgers so that they will fit nicely into the air fryer basket.
2. Preheat the air fryer to 190°C/370°F.
3. If you don't have room for all four burgers, air-fry two or three burgers at a time for 8 minutes. Flip the burgers over and air-fry for another 6 minutes.
4. While the burgers are cooking combine the Dijon mustard, dark brown sugar, and Worcestershire sauce in a small bowl and mix well. This optional topping to the burgers really adds a boost of flavor at the end. Spread the Dijon topping evenly on each burger. If you cooked the burgers in batches, return the first batch to the cooker at this time – it's ok to place the fourth burger on top of the others in the center of the basket. Air-fry the burgers for another 3 minutes.
5. Finally, if desired, top each burger with a slice of Swiss cheese. Lower the air fryer temperature to 165°C/330°F and air-fry for another minute to melt the cheese. Serve the burgers on toasted brioche buns, dressed the way you like them.

Variations & Ingredients Tips:

- Use ground turkey or chicken for a leaner burger option.
- Add minced garlic or finely chopped herbs like parsley or chives for extra flavor.
- Substitute panko breadcrumbs with regular breadcrumbs or oats for a different texture.

Per Serving (1 burger with cheese): Calories: 500; Cholesterol: 120mg; Total Fat: 27g; Saturated Fat: 11g; Sodium: 1180mg; Total Carbohydrates: 21g; Dietary Fiber: 1g; Total Sugars: 5g; Protein: 41g

Eggplant Parmesan Subs

Servings: 2 | Prep Time: 10 Minutes | Cooking Time: 13 Minutes

Ingredients:

- 4 Peeled eggplant slices (about 1.25 cm thick and 7.5 cm in diameter)
- Olive oil spray

- 2 tablespoons plus 2 teaspoons Jarred pizza sauce, any variety except creamy
- ¼ cup (about 20 grams) Finely grated Parmesan cheese
- 2 Small, long soft rolls, such as hero, hoagie, or Italian sub rolls (gluten-free, if a concern), split open lengthwise

Directions:

1. Preheat the air fryer to 175°C/350°F.
2. When the machine is at temperature, coat both sides of the eggplant slices with olive oil spray. Set them in the basket in one layer and air-fry undisturbed for 10 minutes, until lightly browned and softened.
3. Increase the machine's temperature to 190°C/375°F (or 185°C/370°F, if that's the closest setting—unless the machine is already at 180°C/360°F, in which case leave it alone). Top each eggplant slice with 2 teaspoons pizza sauce, then 1 tablespoon of cheese. Air-fry undisturbed for 2 minutes, or until the cheese has melted.
4. Use a nonstick-safe spatula, and perhaps a flatware fork for balance, to transfer the eggplant slices cheese side up to a cutting board. Set the roll(s) cut side down in the basket in one layer (working in batches as necessary) and air-fry undisturbed for 1 minute, to toast the rolls a bit and warm them up. Set 2 eggplant slices in each warm roll.

Variations & Ingredients Tips:

- Use zucchini slices instead of eggplant for a different vegetable option.
- Add a slice of fresh mozzarella on top of the Parmesan for extra cheesiness.
- Sprinkle some dried herbs like oregano or basil on the eggplant before cooking for extra flavor.

Per Serving (1 sandwich): Calories: 280; Cholesterol: 10mg; Total Fat: 9g; Saturated Fat: 3g; Sodium: 840mg; Total Carbohydrates: 40g; Dietary Fiber: 5g; Total Sugars: 8g; Protein: 11g

Sausage And Pepper Heros

Servings: 3 | Prep Time: 10 Minutes | Cooking Time: 11 Minutes

Ingredients:

- 3 links (about 255 grams total) Sweet Italian sausages (gluten-free, if a concern)
- 1½ Medium red or green bell pepper(s), stemmed, cored, and cut into 1.25-cm-wide strips
- 1 medium Yellow or white onion(s), peeled, halved, and sliced into thin half-moons
- 3 Long soft rolls, such as hero, hoagie, or Italian sub rolls (gluten-free, if a concern), split open lengthwise
- For garnishing Balsamic vinegar
- For garnishing Fresh basil leaves

Directions:

1. Preheat the air fryer to 200°C/400°F.
2. When the machine is at temperature, set the sausage links in the basket in one layer and air-fry undisturbed for 5 minutes.
3. Add the pepper strips and onions. Continue air-frying, tossing and rearranging everything about once every minute, for 5 minutes, or until the sausages are browned and an instant-read meat thermometer inserted into one of the links registers 70°C/160°F.
4. Use a nonstick-safe spatula and kitchen tongs to transfer the sausages and vegetables to a cutting board. Set the rolls cut side down in the basket in one layer (working in batches as necessary) and air-fry undisturbed for 1 minute, to toast the rolls a bit and warm them up. Set 1 sausage with some pepper strips and onions in each warm roll, sprinkle balsamic vinegar over the sandwich fillings, and garnish with basil leaves.

Variations & Ingredients Tips:

- Use hot Italian sausage or chorizo for a spicier sandwich.
- Add sliced mushrooms or zucchini to the pepper and onion mixture for extra veggies.
- Top with shredded mozzarella or provolone cheese for a cheesy twist.

Per Serving (1 sandwich): Calories: 560; Cholesterol: 60mg; Total Fat: 36g; Saturated Fat: 12g; Sodium: 1420mg; Total Carbohydrates: 39g; Dietary Fiber: 3g; Total Sugars: 7g; Protein: 24g

Chili Cheese Dogs

Servings: 3 | Prep Time: 10 Minutes | Cooking Time: 12 Minutes

Ingredients:

- 340 grams Lean ground beef
- 1½ tablespoons Chile powder
- 240 grams plus 2 tablespoons Jarred sofrito
- 3 Hot dogs (gluten-free, if a concern)
- 3 Hot dog buns (gluten-free, if a concern), split open lengthwise
- 3 tablespoons Finely chopped scallion
- 60 grams Shredded Cheddar cheese

Directions:

1. Crumble the ground beef into a medium or large saucepan set over medium heat. Brown well, stirring often to break up the clumps. Add the chile powder and cook for 30 seconds, stirring the whole time. Stir in the sofrito and bring to a simmer. Reduce the heat to low and simmer, stirring occasionally, for 5 minutes. Keep warm.
2. Preheat the air fryer to 200°C/400°F.
3. When the machine is at temperature, put the hot dogs in the

basket and air-fry undisturbed for 10 minutes, or until the hot dogs are bubbling and blistered, even a little crisp.

4. Use kitchen tongs to put the hot dogs in the buns. Top each with about 120 grams of the ground beef mixture, 1 tablespoon of the minced scallion, and 20 grams of the cheese. (The scallion should go under the cheese so it superheats and wilts a bit.) Set the filled hot dog buns in the basket and air-fry undisturbed for 2 minutes, or until the cheese has melted.
5. Remove the basket from the machine. Cool the chili cheese dogs in the basket for 5 minutes before serving.

Variations & Ingredients Tips:

- Use turkey or veggie hot dogs for a healthier option.
- Substitute cheddar cheese with your favorite melty cheese, such as pepper jack or Swiss.
- Add diced onions or jalapeños to the chili for extra flavor and heat.

Per Serving: Calories: 580; Cholesterol: 110mg; Total Fat: 32g; Saturated Fat: 13g; Sodium: 1420mg; Total Carbohydrates: 36g; Dietary Fiber: 5g; Total Sugars: 6g; Protein: 38g

Chicken Apple Brie Melt

Servings: 3 | Prep Time: 10 Minutes | Cooking Time: 13 Minutes

Ingredients:

- 3 140 to 170-gram boneless skinless chicken breasts
- Vegetable oil spray
- 1½ teaspoons Dried herbes de Provence
- 85 grams Brie, rind removed, thinly sliced
- 6 Thin cored apple slices
- 3 French rolls (gluten-free, if a concern)
- 2 tablespoons Dijon mustard (gluten-free, if a concern)

Directions:

1. Preheat the air fryer to 190°C/375°F .
2. Lightly coat all sides of the chicken breasts with vegetable oil spray. Sprinkle the breasts evenly with the herbes de Provence.
3. When the machine is at temperature, set the breasts in the basket and air-fry undisturbed for 10 minutes.
4. Top the chicken breasts with the apple slices, then the cheese. Air-fry undisturbed for 2 minutes, or until the cheese is melty and bubbling.
5. Use a nonstick-safe spatula and kitchen tongs, for balance, to transfer the breasts to a cutting board. Set the rolls in the basket and air-fry for 1 minute to warm through. (Putting them in the machine without splitting them keeps the insides very soft while the outside gets a little crunchy.)
6. Transfer the rolls to the cutting board. Split them open lengthwise, then spread 1 teaspoon mustard on each cut side. Set a prepared chicken breast on the bottom of a roll and close with its top, repeating as necessary to make additional sandwiches. Serve warm.

Variations & Ingredients Tips:

- Substitute the Brie with Camembert or another soft cheese of your choice.
- Use pears instead of apples for a different flavor profile.
- Add baby spinach or arugula for extra greens and nutrition.

Per Serving: Calories: 510; Cholesterol: 135mg; Total Fat: 19g; Saturated Fat: 8g; Sodium: 670mg; Total Carbohydrates: 41g; Dietary Fiber: 2g; Total Sugars: 6g; Protein: 45g

Chicken Spiedies

Servings: 3 | Prep Time: 15 Minutes (plus Marinating Time) | Cooking Time: 12 Minutes

Ingredients:

- 570 grams Boneless skinless chicken thighs, trimmed of any fat blobs and cut into 5-cm pieces
- 3 tablespoons Red wine vinegar
- 2 tablespoons Olive oil
- 2 tablespoons Minced fresh mint leaves
- 2 tablespoons Minced fresh parsley leaves
- 2 teaspoons Minced fresh dill fronds
- ¾ teaspoon Fennel seeds
- ¾ teaspoon Table salt
- Up to a ¼ teaspoon Red pepper flakes
- 3 Long soft rolls, such as hero, hoagie, or Italian sub rolls (gluten-free, if a concern), split open lengthwise
- 4½ tablespoons Regular or low-fat mayonnaise (not fat-free; gluten-free, if a concern)
- 1½ tablespoons Distilled white vinegar
- 1½ teaspoons Ground black pepper

Directions:

1. Mix the chicken, vinegar, oil, mint, parsley, dill, fennel seeds, salt, and red pepper flakes in a zip-closed plastic bag. Seal, gently massage the marinade ingredients into the meat, and refrigerate for at least 2 hours or up to 6 hours. (Longer than that and the meat can turn rubbery.)
2. Set the plastic bag out on the counter (to make the contents a little less frigid). Preheat the air fryer to 200°C/400°F.
3. When the machine is at temperature, use kitchen tongs to set the chicken thighs in the basket (discard any remaining marinade) and air-fry undisturbed for 6 minutes. Turn the thighs over and continue air-frying undisturbed for 6 minutes more, until well browned, cooked through, and even a little crunchy.
4. Dump the contents of the basket onto a wire rack and cool for 2 or 3 minutes. Divide the chicken evenly between the rolls. Whisk the mayonnaise, vinegar, and black pepper in a small bowl until smooth. Drizzle this sauce over the chicken pieces in the rolls.

Variations & Ingredients Tips:

- Use chicken breast instead of thighs for a leaner option.

- Substitute the herbs with your favorite combination, such as basil, oregano, or thyme.
- Add sliced onions or pickled vegetables for extra crunch and tanginess.

Per Serving: Calories: 710; Cholesterol: 200mg; Total Fat: 44g; Saturated Fat: 8g; Sodium: 1240mg; Total Carbohydrates: 37g; Dietary Fiber: 2g; Total Sugars: 4g; Protein: 45g

Reuben Sandwiches

Servings: 2 | Prep Time: 10 Minutes | Cooking Time: 11 Minutes

Ingredients:

- 225 grams Sliced deli corned beef
- 4 teaspoons Regular or low-fat mayonnaise (not fat-free)
- 4 Rye bread slices
- 2 tablespoons plus 2 teaspoons Russian dressing
- ½ cup Purchased sauerkraut, squeezed by the handful over the sink to get rid of excess moisture
- 55 grams (2 to 4 slices) Swiss cheese slices (optional)

Directions:

1. Set the corned beef in the basket, slip the basket into the machine, and heat the air fryer to 200°C/400°F. Air-fry undisturbed for 3 minutes from the time the basket is put in the machine, just to warm up the meat.
2. Use kitchen tongs to transfer the corned beef to a cutting board. Spread 1 teaspoon mayonnaise on one side of each slice of rye bread, rubbing the mayonnaise into the bread with a small flatware knife.
3. Place the bread slices mayonnaise side down on a cutting board. Spread the Russian dressing over the "dry" side of each slice. For one sandwich, top one slice of bread with the corned beef, sauerkraut, and cheese (if using). For two sandwiches, top two slices of bread each with half of the corned beef, sauerkraut, and cheese (if using). Close the sandwiches with the remaining bread, setting it mayonnaise side up on top.
4. Set the sandwich(es) in the basket and air-fry undisturbed for 8 minutes, or until browned and crunchy.
5. Use a nonstick-safe spatula, and perhaps a flatware fork for balance, to transfer the sandwich(es) to a cutting board. Cool for 2 or 3 minutes before slicing in half and serving.

Variations & Ingredients Tips:

- Substitute corned beef with pastrami for a classic New York deli taste.
- Use Thousand Island dressing instead of Russian dressing for a tangy, sweet flavor.
- Add sliced dill pickles or mustard to the sandwich for extra zing.

Per Serving (1 sandwich): Calories: 520; Cholesterol: 75mg; Total Fat: 30g; Saturated Fat: 9g; Sodium: 2020mg; Total Carbohydrates: 36g; Dietary Fiber: 4g; Total Sugars: 6g; Protein: 29g

Provolone Stuffed Meatballs

Servings: 4 | Prep Time: 20 Minutes | Cooking Time: 12 Minutes

Ingredients:

- 1 tablespoon olive oil
- 1 small onion, very finely chopped
- 1 to 2 cloves garlic, minced
- 340 grams ground beef
- 340 grams ground pork
- ¾ cup breadcrumbs
- ¼ cup grated Parmesan cheese
- ¼ cup finely chopped fresh parsley (or 1 tablespoon dried parsley)
- ½ teaspoon dried oregano
- 1½ teaspoons salt
- freshly ground black pepper
- 2 eggs, lightly beaten
- 140 grams sharp or aged provolone cheese, cut into 2.5-cm cubes

Directions:

1. Preheat a skillet over medium-high heat. Add the oil and cook the onion and garlic until tender, but not browned.
2. Transfer the onion and garlic to a large bowl and add the beef, pork, breadcrumbs, Parmesan cheese, parsley, oregano, salt, pepper and eggs. Mix well until all the ingredients are combined. Divide the mixture into 12 evenly sized balls. Make one meatball at a time, by pressing a hole in the meatball mixture with your finger and pushing a piece of provolone cheese into the hole. Mold the meat back into a ball, enclosing the cheese.
3. Preheat the air fryer to 190°C/380°F.
4. Working in two batches, transfer six of the meatballs to the air fryer basket and air-fry for 12 minutes, shaking the basket and turning the meatballs a couple of times during the cooking process. Repeat with the remaining six meatballs. You can pop the first batch of meatballs into the air fryer for the last two minutes of cooking to re-heat them. Serve warm.

Variations & Ingredients Tips:

- Substitute beef and pork with ground turkey or chicken for a leaner meatball option.
- Use mozzarella or fontina cheese instead of provolone for a milder flavor.
- Serve meatballs with marinara sauce, in sub rolls, or over pasta for a complete meal.

Per Serving (3 meatballs): Calories: 520; Cholesterol: 180mg; Total Fat: 36g; Saturated Fat: 15g; Sodium: 1160mg; Total Carbohydrates: 18g; Dietary Fiber: 1g; Total Sugars: 2g; Protein: 35g

Best-ever Roast Beef Sandwiches

Servings: 6 | Prep Time: 10 Minutes | Cooking Time: 30-50 Minutes

Ingredients:

- 2½ teaspoons Olive oil
- 1½ teaspoons Dried oregano
- 1½ teaspoons Dried thyme
- 1½ teaspoons Onion powder
- 1½ teaspoons Table salt
- 1½ teaspoons Ground black pepper
- 1 kg Beef eye of round
- 6 Round soft rolls, such as Kaiser rolls or hamburger buns (gluten-free, if a concern), split open lengthwise
- ¾ cup Regular, low-fat, or fat-free mayonnaise (gluten-free, if a concern)
- 6 Romaine lettuce leaves, rinsed
- 6 Round tomato slices (0.5 cm thick)

Directions:

1. Preheat the air fryer to 180°C/350°F .
2. Mix the oil, oregano, thyme, onion powder, salt, and pepper in a small bowl. Spread this mixture all over the eye of round.
3. When the machine is at temperature, set the beef in the basket and air-fry for 30 to 50 minutes (the range depends on the size of the cut), turning the meat twice, until an instant-read meat thermometer inserted into the thickest piece of the meat registers 55°C/130°F for rare, 60°C/140°F for medium, or 65°C/150°F for well-done.
4. Use kitchen tongs to transfer the beef to a cutting board. Cool for 10 minutes. If serving now, carve into 3-mm-thick slices. Spread each roll with 2 tablespoons mayonnaise and divide the beef slices between the rolls. Top with a lettuce leaf and a tomato slice and serve. Or set the beef in a container, cover, and refrigerate for up to 3 days to make cold roast beef sandwiches anytime.

Variations & Ingredients Tips:

- Experiment with different herbs and spices in the rub, such as garlic powder, paprika, or rosemary.
- Add sliced red onions or pickles for extra flavor and crunch.
- Use leftover roast beef for cold sandwiches or salads.

Per Serving: Calories: 560; Cholesterol: 115mg; Total Fat: 27g; Saturated Fat: 6g; Sodium: 980mg; Total Carbohydrates: 32g; Dietary Fiber: 2g; Total Sugars: 4g; Protein: 47g

Philly Cheesesteak Sandwiches

Servings: 3 | Prep Time: 10 Minutes | Cooking Time: 9 Minutes

Ingredients:

- 340 grams Shaved beef
- 1 tablespoon Worcestershire sauce (gluten-free, if a concern)
- ¼ teaspoon Garlic powder
- ¼ teaspoon Mild paprika
- 6 tablespoons (45 grams) Frozen bell pepper strips (do not thaw)
- 2 slices, broken into rings Very thin yellow or white medium onion slice(s)
- 170 grams (6 to 8 slices) Provolone cheese slices
- 3 Long soft rolls such as hero, hoagie, or Italian sub rolls, or hot dog buns (gluten-free, if a concern), split open lengthwise

Directions:

1. Preheat the air fryer to 200°C/400°F.
2. When the machine is at temperature, spread the shaved beef in the basket, leaving a 1.25-cm perimeter around the meat for good air flow. Sprinkle the meat with the Worcestershire sauce, paprika, and garlic powder. Spread the peppers and onions on top of the meat.
3. Air-fry undisturbed for 6 minutes, or until cooked through. Set the cheese on top of the meat. Continue air-frying undisturbed for 3 minutes, or until the cheese has melted.
4. Use kitchen tongs to divide the meat and cheese layers in the basket between the rolls or buns. Serve hot.

Variations & Ingredients Tips:

- Use thinly sliced ribeye or sirloin steak instead of shaved beef for a more traditional texture.
- Add sliced mushrooms to the pepper and onion mixture for extra flavor and nutrition.
- Substitute provolone with American cheese or Cheez Whiz for a classic Philly taste.

Per Serving: Calories: 620; Cholesterol: 135mg; Total Fat: 32g; Saturated Fat: 15g; Sodium: 1320mg; Total Carbohydrates: 38g; Dietary Fiber: 2g; Total Sugars: 5g; Protein: 48g

Chicken Gyros

Servings: 4 | Prep Time: 10 Minutes (plus Marinating Time) | Cooking Time: 14 Minutes

Ingredients:

- 4 110to 140-gram boneless skinless chicken thighs, trimmed of any fat blobs
- 2 tablespoons Lemon juice
- 2 tablespoons Red wine vinegar
- 2 tablespoons Olive oil
- 2 teaspoons Dried oregano
- 2 teaspoons Minced garlic
- 1 teaspoon Table salt
- 1 teaspoon Ground black pepper
- 4 Pita pockets (gluten-free, if a concern)
- ½ cup Chopped tomatoes
- ½ cup Bottled regular, low-fat, or fat-free ranch dressing (gluten-free, if a concern)

Directions:

1. Mix the thighs, lemon juice, vinegar, oil, oregano, garlic, salt, and pepper in a zip-closed bag. Seal, gently massage the marinade into the meat through the plastic, and refrigerate for at least 2 hours or up to 6 hours. (Longer than that and the meat can turn rubbery.)
2. Set the plastic bag out on the counter (to make the contents a little less frigid). Preheat the air fryer to 190°C/375°F.
3. When the machine is at temperature, use kitchen tongs to place the thighs in the basket in one layer. Discard the marinade. Air-fry the chicken thighs undisturbed for 12 minutes, or until browned and an instant-read meat thermometer inserted into the thickest part of one thigh registers 75°C/165°F. You may need to air-fry the chicken 2 minutes longer if the machine's temperature is 70°C/360°F.
4. Use kitchen tongs to transfer the thighs to a cutting board. Cool for 5 minutes, then set one thigh in each of the pita pockets. Top each with 2 tablespoons chopped tomatoes and 2 tablespoons dressing. Serve warm.

Variations & Ingredients Tips:

- Substitute chicken thighs with chicken breast for a leaner option.
- Add shredded lettuce, sliced onions, or cucumbers for extra crunch and flavor.
- Use homemade tzatziki sauce instead of ranch dressing for a more authentic taste.

Per Serving: Calories: 460; Cholesterol: 95mg; Total Fat: 28g; Saturated Fat: 5g; Sodium: 1070mg; Total Carbohydrates: 29g; Dietary Fiber: 2g; Total Sugars: 4g; Protein: 25g

Desserts And Sweets

Maple Cinnamon Cheesecake

Servings: 4 | Prep Time: 15 Minutes | Cooking Time: 12 Minutes

Ingredients:

- 6 sheets of cinnamon graham crackers
- 2 tablespoons butter
- 225-g Neufchâtel cream cheese
- 3 tablespoons pure maple syrup
- 1 large egg
- 1/2 teaspoon ground cinnamon
- 1/4 teaspoon salt

Directions:

1. Preheat air fryer to 175°C/350°F.
2. Crush graham crackers into crumbs. Mix with butter and press into a parchment-lined pan.
3. Air fry crust for 4 minutes.
4. In a bowl, beat cream cheese and maple syrup until smooth.
5. Mix in egg, cinnamon and salt until combined.
6. Pour batter over crust.
7. Reduce heat to 155°C/315°F and bake for 18 mins until set.
8. Refrigerate cheesecake for 3+ hours before serving.

Variations & Ingredients Tips:

- Use mascarpone cheese instead of cream cheese.
- Add chopped pecans or walnuts to the crust.
- Drizzle with extra maple syrup before serving.

Per Serving: Calories: 325; Total Fat: 20g; Saturated Fat: 10g; Sodium: 381mg; Total Carbohydrates: 30g; Dietary Fiber: 1g; Total Sugars: 16g; Protein: 7g

Chocolate Bars

Servings: 4 | Prep Time: 10 Minutes | Cooking Time: 30 Minutes

Ingredients:

- 2 tbsp chocolate toffee chips
- 1/4 cup chopped pecans
- 2 tbsp raisins
- 1 tbsp dried blueberries
- 2 tbsp maple syrup
- 1/4 cup light brown sugar
- 1/3 cup peanut butter
- 2 tbsp chocolate chips
- 2 tbsp butter, melted
- 1/2 tsp vanilla extract
- Salt to taste

Directions:

1. Preheat air fryer at 175°C/350°F.
2. In a bowl, combine all ingredients until well mixed.
3. Press mixture into a lightly greased cake pan and cover with foil.
4. Place pan in air fryer basket and bake for 15 minutes.
5. Remove foil and bake 5 more minutes.
6. Let cool completely for 15 minutes.
7. Turn out onto a plate and cut into 4 bars.

Variations & Ingredients Tips:

- Use different nut varieties like almonds or walnuts.
- Substitute dried cranberries or cherries for raisins.
- Drizzle with melted chocolate or caramel before cutting.

Per Serving (1 bar): Calories: 439; Total Fat: 27g; Saturated Fat: 8g; Sodium: 176mg; Total Carbohydrates: 47g; Dietary Fiber: 4g; Total Sugars: 32g; Protein: 8g

Guilty Chocolate Cookies

Servings: 6 | Prep Time: 10 Minutes | Cooking Time: 25 Minutes

Ingredients:

- 3 eggs, beaten
- 1 tsp vanilla extract
- 1 tsp apple cider vinegar
- 1/3 cup butter, softened
- 1/3 cup sugar
- ¼ cup cacao powder
- ¼ tsp baking soda

Directions:

1. Preheat air fryer to 150°C/300°F.
2. Combine eggs, vanilla extract, and apple vinegar in a bowl until well combined. Refrigerate for 5 minutes.
3. Whisk in butter and sugar until smooth, finally toss in cacao powder and baking soda until smooth.
4. Make balls out of the mixture. Place the balls onto the parchment-lined air fryer basket.
5. Bake for 13 minutes until brown.
6. Using a fork, flatten each cookie. Let cool completely before serving.

Variations & Ingredients Tips:

- Add chocolate chips, chopped nuts, or dried fruit to the dough for extra texture.
- Use coconut sugar or maple syrup instead of regular sugar for a healthier option.
- Serve with a glass of cold milk or a scoop of vanilla ice cream.

Per Serving: Calories: 220; Total Fat: 14g; Saturated Fat: 8g; Sodium: 140mg; Total Carbohydrates: 20g; Dietary Fiber: 2g; Total Sugars: 15g; Protein: 5g

Mixed Berry Hand Pies

Servings: 4 | Prep Time: 15 Minutes | Cooking Time: 15 Minutes

Ingredients:

- 3/4 cup sugar
- 1/2 teaspoon ground cinnamon
- 1 tablespoon cornstarch
- 1 cup blueberries
- 1 cup blackberries
- 1 cup raspberries, divided
- 1 teaspoon water
- 1 package refrigerated pie dough (or your own homemade pie dough)
- 1 egg, beaten

Directions:

1. Combine sugar, cinnamon, cornstarch, blueberries, blackberries and 1/2 cup raspberries in a saucepan. Add water.
2. Cook over medium-high heat for 5 mins until berries break down.
3. Remove from heat, stir in remaining 1/2 cup raspberries and let cool.
4. Preheat air fryer to 190°C/370°F.
5. Cut dough into 10x13-cm and 10x15-cm circles.
6. Place filling on 15-cm circles. Brush edges with water and top with 13-cm circles, crimping to seal.
7. Brush pies with egg wash and vent the tops.
8. Air fry 2 at a time for 9 mins. Flip and cook 6 more mins.
9. Serve warm or at room temp.

Variations & Ingredients Tips:

- Use store-bought or homemade pie filling instead.
- Sprinkle pies with coarse sugar before baking.
- Substitute other fruit like cherry or apple for fillings.

Per Serving: Calories: 286; Total Fat: 6g; Saturated Fat: 2g; Sodium: 137mg; Total Carbohydrates: 57g; Dietary Fiber: 4g; Total Sugars: 34g; Protein: 3g

Strawberry Pastry Rolls

Servings: 4 | Prep Time: 20 Minutes | Cooking Time: 6 Minutes

Ingredients:

- 85-g low-fat cream cheese
- 2 tablespoons plain yogurt
- 2 teaspoons sugar
- 1/4 teaspoon pure vanilla extract
- 225-g fresh strawberries
- 8 sheets phyllo dough
- Butter-flavored cooking spray
- 1/4–1/2 cup dark chocolate chips (optional)

Directions:

1. In a bowl, combine cream cheese, yogurt, sugar, vanilla. Beat until smooth, 1 min.
2. Wash berries, destem. Chop enough for 1/2 cup. Stir into cheese mix.
3. Preheat air fryer to 165°C/330°F.
4. Cover phyllo sheets with waxed paper and damp towel. Remove 1 at a time as using.
5. For 1 roll: Lay 1 sheet phyllo, spray with butter spray, top with 2nd sheet, spray again.
6. Place 1/4 filling (3 tbsp) 1.3cm from short edge. Fold over filling, roll up, folding in sides. Spray outside with butter spray.
7. Place 4 rolls in basket, seam-down, spaced apart. Cook at 165°C/330°F for 6 mins until golden.
8. Repeat with remaining rolls.

9. Let cool. Slice remaining berries. Melt chocolate if using.
10. Top pastries with berries, drizzle with chocolate.

Variations & Ingredients Tips:

- Use other fresh berries.
- Dust with powdered sugar instead of chocolate.
- Stuff with cream cheese or nutella filling.

Per Serving: Calories: 185; Total Fat: 8g; Saturated Fat: 4g; Cholesterol: 15mg; Sodium: 130mg; Total Carbs: 25g; Dietary Fiber: 2g; Total Sugars: 9g; Protein: 5g

Fried Snickers Bars

Servings:8 | Prep Time: 20 Minutes | Cooking Time: 4 Minutes

Ingredients:

- ⅓ cup All-purpose flour
- 1 Large egg white(s), beaten until foamy
- 1½ cups (170 grams) Vanilla wafer cookie crumbs
- 8 Fun-size (17-gram) Snickers bars, frozen
- Vegetable oil spray

Directions:

1. Preheat the air fryer to 200°C/400°F.
2. Set up and fill three shallow soup plates or small pie plates on your counter: one for the flour, one for the beaten egg white(s), and one for the cookie crumbs.
3. Unwrap the frozen candy bars. Dip one in the flour, turning it to coat on all sides. Gently shake off any excess, then set it in the beaten egg white(s). Turn it to coat all sides, even the ends, then let any excess egg white slip back into the rest. Set the candy bar in the cookie crumbs. Turn to coat on all sides, even the ends. Dip the candy bar back in the egg white(s) a second time, then into the cookie crumbs a second time, making sure you have an even coating all around. Coat the covered candy bar all over with vegetable oil spray. Set aside so you can dip and coat the remaining candy bars.
4. Set the coated candy bars in the basket with as much air space between them as possible. Air-fry undisturbed for 4 minutes, or until golden brown.
5. Remove the basket from the machine and let the candy bars cool in the basket for 10 minutes. Use a nonstick-safe spatula to transfer them to a wire rack and cool for 5 minutes more before chowing down.

Variations & Ingredients Tips:

- Use different candy bars like Milky Way, Twix, or Kit Kat.
- Substitute cookie crumbs with crushed pretzels, corn flakes, or Rice Krispies.
- Drizzle with melted chocolate or caramel sauce before serving.

Per Serving: Calories: 250; Total Fat: 12g; Saturated Fat: 5g; Sodium: 140mg; Total Carbohydrates: 34g; Dietary Fiber: 1g; Total Sugars: 21g; Protein: 3g

Chewy Coconut Cake

Servings: 6 | Prep Time: 15 Minutes | Cooking Time: 18-22 Minutes

Ingredients:

- 3/4 cup plus 2 1/2 tablespoons All-purpose flour
- 3/4 teaspoon Baking powder
- 1/8 teaspoon Table salt
- 7 1/2 tablespoons (1 stick minus 1/2 tablespoon) Butter, at room temperature
- 1/3 cup plus 1 tablespoon Granulated white sugar
- 5 tablespoons Packed light brown sugar
- 5 tablespoons Pasteurized egg substitute, such as Egg Beaters
- 2 teaspoons Vanilla extract
- 1/2 cup Unsweetened shredded coconut
- Baking spray

Directions:

1. Preheat air fryer to 165°C/325°F (or 170°C/330°F).
2. Mix flour, baking powder and salt.
3. Beat butter, white sugar and brown sugar until creamy, 3 mins.
4. Beat in egg substitute/egg and vanilla until smooth.
5. Fold in flour mixture just until moistened. Fold in coconut.
6. Grease a 15cm, 18cm or 20cm round cake pan with baking spray.
7. Spread batter evenly into pan.
8. Air fry for 18 mins (15cm), 20 mins (18cm), 22 mins (20cm) until set in center.
9. Cool in pan 1 hour, then slice into wedges.

Variations & Ingredients Tips:

- Use sweetened shredded coconut for extra sweetness.
- Add lime or orange zest to the batter.
- Top with coconut buttercream frosting.

Per Serving: Calories: 334; Total Fat: 17g; Saturated Fat: 10g; Sodium: 134mg; Total Carbohydrates: 42g; Dietary Fiber: 1g; Total Sugars: 23g; Protein: 4g

Spiced Fruit Skewers

Servings: 4 | Prep Time: 10 Minutes | Cooking Time: 15 Minutes

Ingredients:

- 2 peeled peaches, thickly sliced
- 3 plums, halved and pitted
- 3 peeled kiwi, quartered
- 1 tbsp honey
- 1/2 tsp ground cinnamon
- 1/4 tsp ground allspice

- 1/4 tsp cayenne pepper

Directions:

1. Preheat air fryer to 200°C/400°F.
2. Combine the honey, cinnamon, allspice, and cayenne and set aside.
3. Alternate fruits on 8 bamboo skewers, then brush the fruit with the honey mix.
4. Lay the skewers in the air fryer and Air Fry for 3-5 minutes.
5. Allow to chill for 5 minutes before serving.

Variations & Ingredients Tips:

- Use other fresh fruits like mango, pineapple or grapes.
- Drizzle with chocolate sauce or dust with powdered sugar before serving.
- Add a pinch of chili powder to the spice mix for extra heat.

Per Serving: Calories: 95; Total Fat: 0g; Saturated Fat: 0g; Cholesterol: 0mg; Sodium: 5mg; Total Carbs: 24g; Dietary Fiber: 3g; Total Sugars: 18g; Protein: 1g

One-bowl Chocolate Buttermilk Cake

Servings: 6 | Prep Time: 10 Minutes | Cooking Time: 16-20 Minutes

Ingredients:

- 3/4 cup All-purpose flour
- 1/2 cup Granulated white sugar
- 3 tablespoons Unsweetened cocoa powder
- 1/2 teaspoon Baking soda
- 1/4 teaspoon Table salt
- 1/2 cup Buttermilk
- 2 tablespoons Vegetable oil
- 3/4 teaspoon Vanilla extract
- Baking spray

Directions:

1. Preheat the air fryer to 165°C/325°F (or 170°C/330°F, if that's the closest setting).
2. Stir the flour, sugar, cocoa powder, baking soda, and salt in a large bowl until well combined. Add the buttermilk, oil, and vanilla. Stir just until a thick, grainy batter forms.
3. Use the baking spray to generously coat the inside of a 15cm round cake pan for a small batch, a 18cm round cake pan for a medium batch, or a 20cm round cake pan for a large batch. Scrape and spread the chocolate batter into this pan, smoothing the batter out to an even layer.
4. Set the pan in the basket and air-fry undisturbed for 16 minutes for a 15cm layer, 18 minutes for a 18cm layer, or 20 minutes for a 20cm layer, or until a toothpick or cake tester inserted into the center of the cake comes out clean. Start checking it at the 14-minute mark to know where you are.
5. Use hot pads or silicone baking mitts to transfer the cake pan to a wire rack. Cool for 5 minutes. To unmold, set a cutting board over the baking pan and invert both the board and the pan. Lift the still-warm pan off the cake layer. Set the wire rack on top of the cake layer and invert all of it with the cutting board so that the cake layer is now right side up on the wire rack. Remove the cutting board and continue cooling the cake for at least 10 minutes or to room temperature, about 30 minutes, before slicing into wedges.

Variations & Ingredients Tips:

- Substitute buttermilk with equal parts milk mixed with 1 tsp vinegar or lemon juice.
- Add 1/2 cup chocolate chips or chopped nuts to the batter.
- Top with chocolate frosting or powdered sugar glaze.

Per Serving: Calories: 240; Total Fat: 7g; Saturated Fat: 1g; Cholesterol: 5mg; Sodium: 220mg; Total Carbs: 41g; Dietary Fiber: 2g; Total Sugars: 20g; Protein: 4g

Caramel Apple Crumble

Servings: 6 | Prep Time: 15 Minutes | Cooking Time: 50 Minutes

Ingredients:

- 4 apples, peeled and thinly sliced
- 2 tablespoons sugar
- 1 tablespoon flour
- 1 teaspoon ground cinnamon
- 1/4 teaspoon ground allspice
- Healthy pinch ground nutmeg
- 10 caramel squares, cut into small pieces
- Crumble Topping:
- 3/4 cup rolled oats
- 1/4 cup sugar
- 1/3 cup flour
- 1/4 teaspoon ground cinnamon
- 6 tablespoons butter, melted

Directions:

1. Preheat air fryer to 165°C/330°F.
2. Toss apples with sugar, flour, cinnamon, allspice, nutmeg and caramel pieces.
3. Pour into a 15cm baking dish.
4. Make topping by mixing oats, sugar, flour, cinnamon and melted butter.
5. Top apples with crumble mixture. Cover dish with foil.
6. Air fry for 25 mins, then remove foil and cook 25 more mins.
7. Serve warm, with ice cream or whipped cream if desired.

Variations & Ingredients Tips:

- Use a mixture of baking apples like Honeycrisp and Granny Smith.
- Add chopped pecans or walnuts to the crumble topping.
- Drizzle with extra caramel sauce before serving.

Per Serving: Calories: 365; Total Fat: 14g; Saturated Fat: 7g; Sodium: 86mg; Total Carbohydrates: 60g; Dietary Fiber: 4g;

Total Sugars: 35g; Protein: 3g

Fudgy Brownie Cake

Servings: 6 | Prep Time: 10 Minutes | Cooking Time: 25-35 Minutes

Ingredients:

- 6½ tablespoons All-purpose flour
- ¼ cup plus 1 teaspoon Unsweetened cocoa powder
- ½ teaspoon Baking powder
- ¼ teaspoon Table salt
- 6½ tablespoons Butter, at room temperature
- 9½ tablespoons Granulated white sugar
- 1 egg plus 1 large egg white Large egg(s)
- ¾ teaspoon Vanilla extract
- Baking spray

Directions:

1. Preheat the air fryer to 165°C/325°F (or 165°C/330°F, if that's the closest setting).
2. Mix the flour, cocoa powder, baking powder, and salt in a small bowl until well combined.
3. Using an electric hand mixer at medium speed, beat the butter and sugar in a medium bowl until creamy and smooth, about 3 minutes, occasionally scraping down the inside of the bowl.
4. Beat in the egg(s) and the white or yolk (as necessary), as well as the vanilla, until smooth. Turn off the beaters and add the flour mixture. Beat at low speed until thick and smooth.
5. Use the baking spray to generously coat the inside of a 15-cm round cake pan for a small batch, an 18-cm round cake pan for a medium batch, or a 20-cm round cake pan for a large batch. Scrape and spread the batter into the pan, smoothing the batter out to an even layer.
6. Set the pan in the basket and air-fry for 25 minutes for a 15-cm layer, 30 minutes for an 18-cm layer, or 35 minutes for a 20-cm layer, or until the cake is set but soft to the touch. Start checking it at the 20-minute mark to know where you are.
7. Use hot pads or silicone baking mitts to transfer the cake pan to a wire rack. Cool for at least 1 hour or up to 4 hours. Using a nonstick-safe knife, slice the cake into wedges right in the pan and lift them out one by one.

Variations & Ingredients Tips:

- Add ½ cup of chocolate chips, chopped nuts, or dried fruit to the batter.
- Frost the cooled cake with chocolate ganache or cream cheese frosting.
- Serve with a scoop of vanilla ice cream or a dollop of whipped cream.

Per Serving: Calories: 340; Total Fat: 19g; Saturated Fat: 11g; Sodium: 220mg; Total Carbohydrates: 41g; Dietary Fiber: 2g; Total Sugars: 29g; Protein: 4g

Almond-roasted Pears

Servings: 4 | Prep Time: 10 Minutes | Cooking Time: 15 Minutes

Ingredients:

- Yogurt Topping
- 1 container (142-170g) vanilla Greek yogurt
- 1/4 teaspoon almond flavoring
- 2 whole pears
- 1/4 cup crushed Biscoff cookies (approx. 4 cookies)
- 1 tablespoon sliced almonds
- 1 tablespoon butter

Directions:

1. Stir almond flavoring into yogurt and set aside while preparing pears.
2. Halve each pear and spoon out the core.
3. Place pear halves in air fryer basket.
4. Stir together the cookie crumbs and almonds. Place a quarter of this mixture into the hollow of each pear half.
5. Cut butter into 4 pieces and place one piece on top of crumb mixture in each pear.
6. Cook at 180°C/360°F for 15 minutes or until pears have cooked through but are still slightly firm.
7. Serve pears warm with a dollop of yogurt topping.

Variations & Ingredients Tips:

- Use honey Greek yogurt instead of vanilla.
- Substitute graham cracker crumbs for Biscoff cookies.
- Drizzle with honey or maple syrup before serving.

Per Serving: Calories: 207; Total Fat: 8g; Saturated Fat: 3g; Sodium: 52mg; Total Carbohydrates: 31g; Dietary Fiber: 4g; Total Sugars: 20g; Protein: 5g

Coconut Cream Roll-ups

Servings: 4 | Prep Time: 15 Minutes | Cooking Time: 20 Minutes

Ingredients:

- 1/2 cup cream cheese, softened
- 1 cup fresh raspberries
- 1/4 cup brown sugar
- 1/4 cup coconut cream
- 1 egg
- 1 tsp corn starch
- 6 spring roll wrappers

Directions:

1. Preheat air fryer to 175°C/350°F.
2. Mix cream cheese, brown sugar, coconut cream, cornstarch and egg until fluffy.
3. Spoon filling onto spring roll wrappers and top with raspberries.

4. Roll up wrappers around filling and seal with water.
5. Place seam-side down on foil-lined air fryer basket.
6. Bake for 10 minutes, flipping once, until golden.
7. Remove with tongs and serve hot or cold.

Variations & Ingredients Tips:

- Use other berries like blueberries or strawberries.
- Add shredded coconut to the filling.
- Drizzle with melted white or dark chocolate after baking.

Per Serving: Calories: 247; Total Fat: 13g; Saturated Fat: 8g; Sodium: 167mg; Total Carbohydrates: 28g; Dietary Fiber: 3g; Total Sugars: 15g; Protein: 5g

Molten Chocolate Almond Cakes

Servings: 3 | Prep Time: 15 Minutes | Cooking Time: 13 Minutes

Ingredients:

- Butter and flour for the ramekins
- 115g bittersweet chocolate, chopped
- 1/2 cup (1 stick) unsalted butter
- 2 eggs
- 2 egg yolks
- 1/4 cup sugar
- 1/2 teaspoon pure vanilla or almond extract
- 1 tablespoon all-purpose flour
- 3 tablespoons ground almonds
- 8 to 12 semisweet chocolate discs (or 4 chunks)
- Cocoa powder or powdered sugar, for dusting
- Toasted almonds, coarsely chopped

Directions:

1. Butter and flour three 170g ramekins.
2. Melt chocolate and butter together.
3. In another bowl, beat eggs, yolks and sugar until light and smooth. Add extract.
4. Whisk chocolate mixture into egg mixture.
5. Stir in flour and ground almonds.
6. Preheat air fryer to 165°C/330°F.
7. Fill ramekins halfway with batter. Add chocolate discs/chunks. Top with remaining batter to 1.3cm from top.
8. Air fry for 13 minutes until sides are set but centers slightly soft.
9. Let sit 5 minutes, then unmold onto plates.
10. Dust with cocoa/powdered sugar. Serve with ice cream and chopped toasted almonds.

Variations & Ingredients Tips:

- Use different nuts like hazelnuts or pistachios.
- Add a splash of liqueur like Frangelico.
- Top with caramel or fruit sauce instead of powdered sugar.

Per Serving: Calories: 570; Total Fat: 41g; Saturated Fat: 20g; Sodium: 85mg; Total Carbohydrates: 46g; Dietary Fiber: 4g; Total Sugars: 34g; Protein: 9g

Cherry Hand Pies

Servings: 8 | Prep Time: 20 Minutes | Cooking Time: 8 Minutes

Ingredients:

- 4 cups frozen or canned pitted tart cherries (if using canned, drain and pat dry)
- 2 teaspoons lemon juice
- 1/2 cup sugar
- 1/4 cup cornstarch
- 1 teaspoon vanilla extract
- 1 Basic Pie Dough (see the preceding recipe) or store-bought pie dough

Directions:

1. In a saucepan, cook cherries and lemon juice over medium heat for 10 minutes until cherries break down.
2. Mix sugar and cornstarch, then stir into cherries. Cook 2-3 minutes until thickened.
3. Remove from heat, stir in vanilla and let cool to room temp (30 mins).
4. Divide pie dough into 8 pieces. Roll each into a circle 0.5-cm thick.
5. Place 1/4 cup filling in the center of each circle. Fold into a half-circle and crimp edges with a fork to seal. Prick tops.
6. Preheat air fryer to 175°C/350°F.
7. Place pies in single layer in air fryer basket and spray with cooking spray.
8. Cook for 8-10 minutes until golden brown.

Variations & Ingredients Tips:

- Use other fruit fillings like apple, blueberry or peach.
- Brush tops with egg wash before baking for a shiny finish.
- Dust with powdered sugar or drizzle with glaze after baking.

Per Serving: Calories: 267; Total Fat: 9g; Saturated Fat: 3g; Sodium: 116mg; Total Carbohydrates: 44g; Dietary Fiber: 2g; Total Sugars: 22g; Protein: 3g

Banana-lemon Bars

Servings: 6 | Prep Time: 15 Minutes | Cooking Time: 40 Minutes

Ingredients:

- 3/4 cup flour
- 2 tbsp powdered sugar
- 1/4 cup coconut oil, melted
- 1/2 cup brown sugar
- 1 tbsp lemon zest
- 1/4 cup lemon juice
- 1/8 tsp salt
- 1/4 cup mashed bananas
- 1 3/4 tsp cornstarch
- 3/4 tsp baking powder

Directions:

1. Mix flour, powdered sugar and melted coconut oil. Refrig-

erate.

2. Combine brown sugar, zest, juice, salt, bananas, cornstarch and baking powder.
3. Preheat air fryer to 175°C/350°F. Oil a baking pan.
4. Remove crust from fridge and press into bottom of pan. Air fry 5 mins until firm.
5. Spread lemon-banana filling over crust.
6. Bake for 18-20 mins until top is golden.
7. Cool completely before cutting into bars.

Variations & Ingredients Tips:

- Use gingersnap crumbs in the crust.
- Substitute lime juice and zest for lemon.
- Top with toasted coconut before baking.

Per Serving: Calories: 252; Total Fat: 10g; Saturated Fat: 7g; Sodium: 165mg; Total Carbohydrates: 39g; Dietary Fiber: 2g; Total Sugars: 20g; Protein: 2g

Baked Stuffed Pears

Servings: 4 | Prep Time: 15 Minutes | Cooking Time: 15 Minutes + Cooling Time

Ingredients:

- 4 cored pears, halved
- 1/2 cup chopped cashews
- 1/2 cup dried cranberries
- 1/4 cup agave nectar
- 1/2 stick butter, softened
- 1/2 tsp ground cinnamon
- 1/2 cup apple juice

Directions:

1. Preheat the air fryer to 180°C/350°F.
2. Combine the cashews, cranberries, agave nectar, butter, and cinnamon and mix well.
3. Stuff this mixture into the pears, heaping it up on top.
4. Set the pears in a baking pan and pour the apple juice into the bottom of the pan.
5. Put the pan in the fryer and Bake for 10-12 minutes or until the pears are tender.
6. Let cool before serving.

Variations & Ingredients Tips:

- Use honey or maple syrup instead of agave nectar.
- Add chopped dates or raisins to the stuffing mixture.
- Sprinkle with cinnamon sugar before baking.

Per Serving: Calories: 370; Total Fat: 19g; Saturated Fat: 7g; Sodium: 83mg; Total Carbohydrates: 51g; Dietary Fiber: 7g; Total Sugars: 36g; Protein: 5g

Wild Blueberry Sweet Empanadas

Servings: 12 | Prep Time: 30 Minutes (includes Chilling Jam) | Cooking Time: 8 Minutes

Ingredients:

- 2 cups frozen wild blueberries
- 5 tablespoons chia seeds
- 1/4 cup honey
- 1 tablespoon lemon or lime juice
- 1/4 cup water
- 1 1/2 cups all-purpose flour
- 1 cup whole-wheat flour
- 1/2 teaspoon salt
- 1 tablespoon sugar
- 1/2 cup cold unsalted butter
- 1 egg
- 1/2 cup plus 2 tablespoons milk, divided
- 1 cup powdered sugar
- 1 teaspoon vanilla extract

Directions:

1. To make the wild blueberry chia jam, place the blueberries, chia seeds, honey, lemon or lime juice, and water into a blender and pulse for 2 minutes. Pour the chia jam into a glass jar or bowl and cover. Store in the refrigerator at least 4 to 8 hours or until the jam is thickened.
2. In a food processor, place the all-purpose flour, whole-wheat flour, salt, sugar, and butter and process for 2 minutes, scraping down the sides of the food processor every 30 seconds. Add in the egg and blend for 30 seconds. Using the pulse button, add in 1/2 cup of the milk 1 tablespoon at a time or until the dough is moist enough to handle and be rolled into a ball. Let the dough rest at room temperature for 30 minutes.
3. On a floured surface, cut the dough in half; then form a ball and cut each ball into 6 equal pieces, totaling 12 equal pieces. Work with one piece at a time, and cover the remaining dough with a towel. Roll out the dough into a 15cm round, with 6mm thickness. Place 4 tablespoons of filling in the center of round, fold over to form a half-circle. Using a fork, crimp the edges together and pierce the top with a fork for air holes. Repeat with the remaining dough and filling.
4. Preheat the air fryer to 175°C/350°F.
5. Working in batches, place 3 to 4 empanadas in the air fryer basket and spray with cooking spray. Cook for 8 minutes. Repeat in batches, as needed. Allow the sweet empanadas to cool for 15 minutes.
6. Meanwhile, in a small bowl, whisk together the powdered sugar, the remaining 2 tablespoons of milk, and the vanilla extract. Then drizzle the glaze over the surface and serve.

Variations & Ingredients Tips:

- Use other berry varieties like raspberries or blackberries.
- Dust with cinnamon-sugar before baking.
- Serve with vanilla ice cream or whipped cream.

Per Serving (1 empanada): Calories: 265; Total Fat: 11g; Saturated Fat: 6g; Cholesterol: 35mg; Sodium: 115mg; Total Carbs: 39g; Dietary Fiber: 4g; Total Sugars: 16g; Protein: 5g

Carrot Cake With Cream Cheese Icing

Servings: 6 | Prep Time: 30 Minutes | Cooking

Time: 55 Minutes

Ingredients:

- 1 ¼ cups all-purpose flour
- 1 teaspoon baking powder
- ½ teaspoon baking soda
- 1 teaspoon ground cinnamon
- ¼ teaspoon ground nutmeg
- ¼ teaspoon salt
- 2 cups grated carrot (about 3 to 4 medium carrots or 2 large)
- ¾ cup granulated sugar
- ¼ cup brown sugar
- 2 eggs
- ¾ cup canola or vegetable oil
- For the icing:
- 227 grams cream cheese, softened at room temperature
- 113 grams butter (110-g or 1 stick), softened at room temperature
- 1 cup powdered sugar
- 1 teaspoon pure vanilla extract

Directions:

1. Grease a 18-cm cake pan.
2. Combine the flour, baking powder, baking soda, cinnamon, nutmeg and salt in a bowl. Add the grated carrots and toss well.
3. In a separate bowl, beat the sugars and eggs together until light and frothy. Drizzle in the oil, beating constantly. Fold the egg mixture into the dry ingredients until everything is just combined and you no longer see any traces of flour.
4. Pour the batter into the cake pan and wrap the pan completely in greased aluminum foil.
5. Preheat the air fryer to 180°C/350°F.
6. Lower the cake pan into the air fryer basket using a sling made of aluminum foil (fold a piece of aluminum foil into a strip about 5-cm wide by 60-cm long). Fold the ends of the aluminum foil into the air fryer, letting them rest on top of the cake. Air-fry for 40 minutes. Remove the aluminum foil cover and air-fry for an additional 15 minutes or until a skewer inserted into the center of the cake comes out clean and the top is nicely browned.
7. While the cake is cooking, beat the cream cheese, butter, powdered sugar and vanilla extract together using a hand mixer, stand mixer or food processor (or a lot of elbow grease!).
8. Remove the cake pan from the air fryer and let the cake cool in the cake pan for 10 minutes or so. Then remove the cake from the pan and let it continue to cool completely.
9. Frost the cake with the cream cheese icing and serve.

Variations & Ingredients Tips:

- Add ½ cup of raisins, chopped walnuts, or pecans to the batter.
- Substitute ¼ cup of the oil with unsweetened applesauce for a lower fat version.
- Use a lemon cream cheese frosting for a tangy twist.

Per Serving: Calories: 740; Total Fat: 49g; Saturated Fat: 20g; Sodium: 470mg; Total Carbohydrates: 71g; Dietary Fiber: 2g; Total Sugars: 49g; Protein: 8g

Fall Caramelized Apples

Servings: 2 | Prep Time: 5 Minutes | Cooking Time: 25 Minutes

Ingredients:

- 2 apples, sliced
- 1 ½ tsp brown sugar
- ¼ tsp cinnamon
- ¼ tsp nutmeg
- ¼ tsp salt
- 1 tsp lemon zest

Directions:

1. Preheat air fryer to 200°C/390°F.
2. Set the apples upright in a baking pan. Add 2 tbsp of water to the bottom to keep the apples moist.
3. Sprinkle the tops with sugar, lemon zest, cinnamon, and nutmeg. Lightly sprinkle the halves with salt and the tops with oil.
4. Bake for 20 minutes or until the apples are tender and golden on top.
5. Enjoy.

Variations & Ingredients Tips:

- Use pears, peaches, or plums instead of apples.
- Add a scoop of vanilla ice cream or a dollop of whipped cream on top.
- Sprinkle with granola or chopped nuts for extra crunch.

Per Serving: Calories: 120; Total Fat: 0g; Saturated Fat: 0g; Sodium: 300mg; Total Carbohydrates: 32g; Dietary Fiber: 5g; Total Sugars: 25g; Protein: 0g

INDEX

Q

R

S

T

V

W

Z

Printed in Great Britain
by Amazon

53959045R00051